Looking at History

R J Unstead

Looking at History

Adam & Charles Black   London

Published by A & C Black Ltd
35 Bedford Row London WC1R 4JH

ISBN 0 7136 1572 9

First published in this edition 1975
Reprinted 1976 and 1978
© 1975 A & C Black Ltd
Previous editions © 1955, 1963, 1966 A & C Black Ltd

Additional acknowledgements: Trustees of the
British Museum v, index page iv; Mary Evans
Picture Library iv, vii; Radio Times Hulton
Picture Library iii.

Printed in Great Britain by Sir Joseph Causton & Sons Ltd
London and Eastleigh

Contents

A complete list of the contents of each part will be found at the beginning of each of the five parts.

Introduction

This book is about the everyday lives of people in Britain from the days when they lived in caves to the present day. It tells how they built their homes and furnished them, cooked their food, worked for a living, played games and enjoyed themselves, dressed, fought and travelled by land, by sea and, recently, by air.

There is not much about kings, queens, battles and politics, only just enough to let you know who were the rulers and what were the chief events at the time when, say, people lived on the manor or rode in stage coaches.

Because I believe that pictures are a great help in understanding history, there are over 1100 illustrations in this book, very many of them in full colour. Some have come from contemporary sources, such as old books and prints, others have been specially drawn and, for recent times, there are photographs. I hope they will help you to enjoy 'looking at history'.

RJ Unstead

How the book is arranged

Looking at History is made up of five parts. Each part is a book in its own right and has its own index. At the end of *Looking at History* you will find a complete index, so that if, for example, you want to find out about ships through the ages, you will be able to look up Roman ships or Tudor ships from the same index entry.

Looking at History   R J Unstead

Book One

From Cavemen to Vikings

Adam and Charles Black   London

A Roman Mosaic

Published by A & C Black Ltd
35 Bedford Row, London WC1R 4JH

ISBN 0 7136 1420 X limp
    0 7136 1416 1 net
    0 7136 1572 9 complete edition of Books 1–5

First published in this edition 1974   Reprinted 1975
Reprinted 1975, 1977 and 1978
© 1974 A & C Black Ltd
Previous editions © 1953, 1971 A & C Black Ltd

Printed in Great Britain by Sir Joseph Causton & Sons Ltd
London and Eastleigh

Contents

An ivory casket, about AD 700

Acknowledgements

A–Z Botanical Collections Ltd 22
Aerofilms Ltd 27, 36b
Ashmolean Museum, Oxford 58b
Trustees of the British Museum 3, 13, 18a & b, 19a, b & c, 23a, b & c, 26a, 29, 31, 33a & b, 34, 35, 36a, c & d, 38a & b, 41a, b & c, 42, 43, 44a & b, 45a & b, 47, 50, 51a & b, 52, 54b & c, 57a, 58a, 59a, 60b, 63b, title page, cover
Henry Cooper & Son 63c
Department of the Environment 4, 14, 17, 20
French Government Tourist Office 11a & b
Guildhall Museum 45c
Trustees of the London Museum 26b, 36e, 37a & b
A L Parker 54a
J G Pearson 55b
Sussex Archaeological Trust 2, 39, 40
Swedish National Travel Association 59c
Trinity College, Cambridge 55a
Universitetets Oldsaksamling, Oslo 57b, 59b
Illustration 60a is reproduced by kind permission of the City of Bayeux
Drawings in this book are by Doreen Roberts and J C B Knight
Designed by Karen Bowen

People in the Old Stone Age 1

Thousands of years ago, Britain was covered with thick forests.

The weather was hot and animals, such as lions, elephants and giant deer, roamed the forests. The hippopotamus and rhinoceros also lived there, and there were other animals, like the great mammoth, the woolly rhinoceros and the sabre-toothed tiger, which have now died out.

Early man

Bones of these animals have been dug up in Britain. Parts of skeletons which, in thousands of years, have become as hard as stone are called fossils.

The first men lived like the animals. They had to hunt for their food and, because they were not very big or swift, they lived on berries, fruits, shell-fish and the meat of any small animals they could catch.

A rhinoceros

A lion

An elephant

A mammoth

A cave home. The woman is scraping a skin so that it can be made into clothes

Early man threw stones to kill his prey

The weather was warm, so early man did not wear any clothes. Mostly, he stayed near to a river or stream and he would hide in the trees when the big animals came to the streams to drink.

Although he was small and weak, early man was cleverer than the animals. He could pick up a stick and use it as a club; he could throw a stone and use its sharp edge to dig or scrape.

When the weather became much colder, animals like the lions and tigers moved away. They could do this because Britain was still joined by land to France.

Early man also felt the cold. He learned to wrap himself in the skin of a dead animal and he looked for somewhere to shelter.

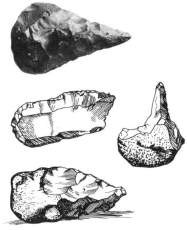

Stone tools

Early man made his first home among the rocks or in a cave. He liked to find a cave near to a river, so that he had water to drink.

Because he had no knives and knew nothing about iron, he used flints for cutting, and he learned how to chip them into many shapes. At first he made a sort of knife called a hand-axe. He held the stone in one hand and chopped downwards with its sharp edge. He also made scrapers and borers to make holes in wood.

His wife used a scraper to clean the inside of animal skins, so that they could be used as clothes and rugs in cold weather.

Because man's only tools were made of stone, this period is called the Stone Age.

Making a fire

Stone Age people found out how to make a fire. They twisted or rubbed a stick in a groove of another piece of wood, until it grew so hot that it set fire to pieces of dry grass and small twigs.

Another way was to strike certain stones together so that sparks flew and set fire to pieces of dry grass. Making fire was probably the woman's job, but the children had to gather sticks to help keep the fire alight.

A fire kept the family warm and it frightened wild animals away from the cave. It was also useful for making one end of a stick hard and sharp.

Cooking meat outside a cave

Cooking may have started when a piece of meat fell near the fire. After this, the woman probably cooked by holding a lump of meat on a stick or by placing it in the hot ashes.

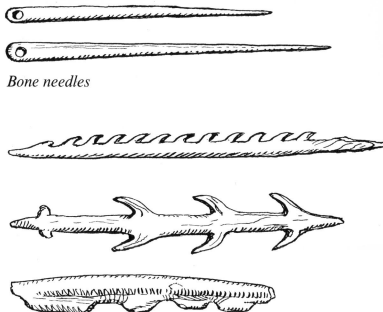

Bone needles

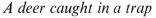

A deer caught in a trap

Harpoon heads made of bone

The cavemen were hunters. They did not yet know how to keep animals or grow crops.

Sometimes the wild animals would move to new feeding-grounds. Then the cavemen and their families would leave the cave and follow them. The hunters went long distances in search of food, living where they could among bushes and rocks. In winter, they went back to the cave.

It was a hard life, having to kill animals for food. The men dug pits and covered them with branches and leaves to trap big animals on their way to water. They would kill the trapped animal with spears, stones and throwing-axes.

In time, they learned how to make bows and arrows.

Animals gave the hunters almost everything they needed—food to eat, skins to wear and splinters of bone for needles and fish-hooks.

An elk

9

They liked fish and went fishing in rivers with a spear. They also used bone fish-hooks on lines made from animal sinews and strong grasses or creepers.

Some families lived by the sea and ate shell-fish which they gathered from the rocks. They left great piles of shells behind.

Early man made his first boat from a fallen log or he cut down a tree near the river with his stone axe. He hollowed out the tree-trunk into the shape of a boat, using an axe or fire to do so.

Fishing with a spear, and using a dug-out canoe

*Cave paintings from France, showing deer and buffalo—
the animals the hunters hoped to find*

In some places, men painted pictures on the walls
of the cave. For paint, they used brown and yellow
earth and soot from the fire.

They painted pictures of the animals they wanted
to kill when out hunting. Animals were very
important to them, so they painted or scratched
the pictures very carefully. It was a kind of magic
to paint these pictures far back in the cave.

Making cave paintings

11

Dogs were trained to hunt

Hundreds of years went by and the weather became warmer. The forests were not quite so dense and the uplands became grassy hills.

Life was not such a bitter struggle, but the hunters still had to spend nearly all their time getting enough to eat.

They now had dogs to help them track and run down the animals. Dogs were the first creatures to be tamed.

The next tame or domestic animals were sheep, cows and pigs. Men began looking after flocks and herds instead of spending all their time hunting.

Keeping animals meant living where there was grass, so the herdsmen avoided the forests and kept to the hills. Since the animals had to move about to find grass, the people moved with them and made shelters for themselves.

The first huts were made of branches and skins

The first huts were made of branches; there was a pole in the middle with long sticks tied to the top and covered with skins. This was a place to sleep in and the fire was made on the ground outside.

The New Stone Age 2

As time went by, men became very clever at making flint tools. They could chip a flint until it was as sharp as a razor, and they gave their tools a fine finish or polish.

To get the best flints, they dug deep into the chalk, using pick-axes made from stag's horns, and they hauled the flints up in baskets from the pits and underground passages.

Some of the men and women learned how to make clay pots and bowls to hold milk. They shaped the clay with their hands and baked the pots in the fire. Some men could make a bowl from a hard stone.

A pick-axe made from a stag's horn

A flint mine

Making clay pots

13

Inside a hut

People still lived by hunting and keeping flocks and herds. Some of them also knew how to grow corn. They scratched the earth with flint hoes and antler-picks, planted seeds and reaped their crops with flint sickles.

Now, they could build huts that lasted longer than shelters made from branches and skins. They dug out a circle about waist-deep and built up a wall of stones, leaving a gap for the door. A post in the middle supported the roof, made of branches covered with turf. The floor inside the hut was lower than the ground outside; this gave more headroom and made the hut less draughty.

The remains of stone huts at Skara Brae on Orkney, Scotland

The fire was made on a flat stone and the smoke went out of a hole in the roof. Some flat stones covered with skins made a seat or a bed.

Where there were no stones, men set up a ring of posts and tied branches from them to a taller pole in the middle. The walls were made of a kind of basket-work called wattle, smeared all over with wet clay. This kept the wind out.

When a group of huts had been built, a long fence was put all round them to keep out wild animals and enemies. Inside the fence were the huts, pens for the animals, hay-ricks and poles for drying grass.

Flocks and herds were brought in at night. Each morning, they were let out to feed on the grassy hills.

Making a hut from wattle smeared over with wet clay

An attack on a hill-fort

People were now living together in family-groups or tribes. Since they now had bowls, tools, weapons, necklaces and animals which another tribe might steal, they needed a chief to give orders and to lead them in battle.

The chief probably owned more animals than the rest and lived in the biggest hut. When he and his followers made war on another tribe, they fought with spears, clubs and stones.

More people were now living in Britain and the tribes were often at war with one another. Some of them built hill-forts. They would shelter from enemies behind ditches and fences placed round the summit of a hill.

The stones at Stonehenge may have been raised into position like this

In the Stone Age men worshipped the sun and the moon. They also believed in spirits which lived in trees, streams and lonely places. They built rings of huge stones for their gods. The most famous one at Stonehenge, is so old that no one is sure how the great stones were brought a great distance to Salisbury Plain.

Tribesmen came great distances to visit this temple, and they travelled there on foot, walking along the tops of the low hills to avoid the wild animals which lived in valleys. A number of grassy tracks led to Stonehenge from distant parts of the country.

Stonehenge, on Salisbury plain

3 People of the Bronze Age

A bronze sword and two knives from Ireland

Bronze axe-heads

Men from the East came to Britain, bringing a metal with them called bronze. This was a mixture of copper and tin, heated together.

Bronze tools and weapons were better than stone implements. They were sharper and they did not break so easily. When a bronze axe or sword became blunt, it could be hammered until it was sharp again.

All kinds of bowls, pins, knives, tongs, bracelets and ornaments were made. Bronze-smiths also made spear-heads, shields, axes, trumpets and the first swords. Metal spearheads were fixed into the wooden shaft by a spike, but someone then invented a spearhead with a socket or collar that simply fitted over the shaft and was fixed by two little nails.

Bronze Age men were farmers, though, of course, they still went hunting from time to time.

People of the Bronze Age

A bronze trumpet   *A cauldron*

*A mould for making
a bronze spearhead*

They kept cows and sheep, and were beginning to have horses, too. Boys looked after the pigs on the edge of the forest. To make hay for feeding the animals in winter, farmers cut the long grass and dried it on poles.

With a wooden plough, pulled by oxen, they broke up the earth in their narrow hillside fields and planted corn, mostly barley.

When the ripe corn had been cut, the women ground it between two mill-stones. The lower stone was fixed and had a wooden peg in the middle; the top stone fitted over this and corn, poured through the centre hole, was ground into flour between the upper and lower millstones. Then the women made bread and flat cakes which they cooked on hot stones by the fire.

Grinding corn

*Bronze Age people
spent much of their
time farming*

19

Using a coracle

Inside a Bronze Age barrow

The first chariots had solid wheels

About this time, men learned how to make wheels. The first ones were solid. Later they learned how to make spokes. With a pair of wheels, it was easy to make a cart and then horses were trained to pull war chariots.

The floor of the chariot was made of wood and the sides of basket-work were covered with ox-hide.

To cross rivers and for fishing, tribesmen made round boats of basketwork, covered with skins. These coracles, as they are called, were so light that a man could carry one on his back. You might still see a coracle in Wales or Ireland.

Bronze Age people buried their dead carefully in a pit covered over with a mound of earth or stones. These mounds are called "barrows". Oxen, sheep, horses and dogs were sometimes killed and put in the grave with their dead master.

The Iron Age 4

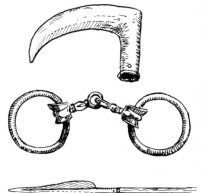

An iron sword

After many more years, some people called Celts came across the sea to Britain, bringing another metal with them. This was iron and it made better weapons and tools than bronze because it was harder.

Since Bronze Age times, people had been making cloth. First, wool had to be twisted into long threads. This was spinning and it was done by the girls, as shown in the picture.

The stick in the girl's right hand is called the spindle and the round weight at the end is the whorl. On her shoulder is the distaff with a roll of wool. She twists the wool in her fingers until she has a piece long enough to tie to the spindle stick, which spins round and round to twist the wool into thread.

The threads were made into cloth by fixing them down on a frame to keep them straight; then the girl wove other threads in and out across the frame. In this way, she made a woollen cloth. This is called weaving.

Spinning with a distaff

Weaving on a loom

21

A finer cloth called linen, was made from flax, a plant with pretty blue flowers and a woody stem. When the stems were soaked in water and dried in the sun, girls could pick out the silky part of the stems and spin it into thread.

They dyed the linen and woollen cloth with dyes made from plants and tree bark. They loved bright colours, especially blues and reds.

At first, people simply wrapped a piece of cloth round them and fastened it with pins and brooches. A belt with a bronze buckle was worn round the waist.

Women also wore a blouse, with short sleeves and a slit for the head. It was made of one piece of cloth and was sewn down the back. With the blouse, they wore a skirt, usually long, but sometimes to the knees.

Men wore a short tunic, woollen cap and cloak. Sometimes the tunic had no top or sleeves, but just two leather straps over the shoulders.

Both men and women wore shoes made of soft leather, with straps crossed round the ankles.

Iron was used to make tools and weapons, but bronze was still the metal for every kind of ornament. Buckles, brooches, cloak-pins and hand-mirrors were beautifully made, and great pride was taken in the chief's shield and helmet, and in the harness ornaments for his chariot-horses.

Metal workers added studs of red enamel and patterns of coral to decorate the shining bronze. Gold, which was found in Britain at this time, was also used for ornaments.

Gold ornaments found at Ipswich in Suffolk

A jug and a mirror, made of bronze during the Iron Age

23

Lake dwellers

To protect themselves from enemies, some people made their homes in the marshes and lakes. One of these lake villages was built at Glastonbury, where a muddy island in a lake was raised by piling up earth. This was kept in position with poles and tree-trunks driven into the mud.

On this earth floor, the Glastonbury people built a village of 80 or 90 round wattle huts. Each hut had a pole in the middle to hold up the roof and a flat hearth-stone on the floor. When this heavy stone sank into the soft ground, another one was put on top. As many as nine or ten hearth-stones have been found, one on top of another.

The lake village at Glastonbury

All round the island was a fence to keep out enemies, and the lake-people went ashore every morning in their flat-bottomed boats to work in the fields and look after their animals. They came back to the island in the evening.

Tools of stone, bronze and iron have been found at Glastonbury. There were knives, axes, sickles, saws, chisels, nails, rings, harness-fittings and chariot-wheels, but, apart from a few daggers, swords and spearheads, not many weapons. Perhaps this was why the lake-dwellers could not beat off their enemies. In the end, the village was attacked and its people put to the sword.

5   The Ancient Britons

When we talk of the Ancient Britons, we usually mean the people who were living in the island not long before the Romans came.

These Ancient Britons were the same kind of people as the Celts who first brought iron to Britain. They lived in tribes under a chief, a king or a queen. These tribes were constantly at war with one another.

Their homes were wattle-and-daub huts, often grouped together in a strong place, surrounded by a wooden fence and a ditch.

The Ancient Britons loved bright colours and fine metalwork. The men wore tartan kilts or long loose trousers, helmets and cloaks. The women dressed in short-sleeved garments, plaited their hair and, like the men, were very fond of bracelets and jewellery.

A bronze helmet found in the River Thames

An Iron Age village at Heathrow – where London Airport is now

Working the fields around a hill-fort

The remains of a hill-fort today

Besides fighting, the Britons were good at farming. They kept cattle and sheep, and tilled their narrow fields which often ran round the sides of a hill. The land in the valleys was too damp and heavy for their light ploughs.

On the hill-tops, they built forts, often enlarging the old Bronze Age forts with new ditches and fences, and with strong entrance gates to baffle their enemies.

Men now began to have special jobs. Some would work as shepherds or bee-keepers, as smiths or makers of harness or ploughs or barrels. There were rich chiefs, warriors, poor workers and slaves captured in battle.

Traders from the Mediterranean barter with the Britons

Some men were traders. They travelled along the grassy tracks to buy and sell goods such as cloth, corn, tin, skins, pottery and ornaments.

Much of the trading was by barter, that is, a sheep would be exchanged for a bracelet or piece of cloth. But iron bars and gold coins were also used. Some of the traders went by boat to Gaul – the old name for France. The Britons were friendly with the Gauls.

Traders from the Mediterranean sailed to the coasts of Britain to buy tin and gold, slaves, hunting-dogs and skins. They brought beautiful cloths, pottery, beads and weapons in exchange.

Iron currency bars

Phoenicians building a ship

Some of these traders were called Phoenicians. They came from Carthage in North Africa and were the greatest sea-traders before the Romans. They not only reached Britain but sailed on as far as the Baltic Sea to buy amber, which was much prized for ornaments.

Greek traders also came to Britain, which they called the Tin Islands. About 300 years before Christ, a Greek called Pytheas sailed round the islands and took home stories of a people living in a rainy land where they dug and smelted tin, grew wheat and drank a strange drink made from barley and honey.

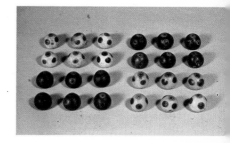

Counters for playing a game. The game was probably rather like Ludo and the counters may have come from abroad

29

The Druids made human sacrifices

A Roman galley

The Britons worshipped many gods and goddesses of nature and battle. The human head seemed very important to them and they would hang up the heads of enemies in their temples. They sometimes drank out of cups made of wood or stone in the shape of a head.

Their priests or wise men were called Druids and they looked on the oak-tree and mistletoe as sacred. When, on special occasions, the mistletoe was cut, white bulls and even human beings were killed as sacrifices.

Stonehenge and other stone circles were still holy places. They had been raised long before the time of the Druids. The island of Anglesey, off North Wales, was the Druids' holy place.

When the Romans came to Britain, they found that the Druids had great power in the land, so they marched to Anglesey, killed the Druids and destroyed the sacred groves of oak trees.

The Romans 6

Fifty-five years before Jesus was born, a Roman army came to Britain.

The Britons had been helping their friends in Gaul to fight against Julius Caesar, the Roman general. Caesar decided that he would punish the Britons and he also wanted to see the mysterious Tin Islands for himself.

He sailed across the Channel with a strong force of soldiers who landed on the coast, fought their way ashore and defeated the Britons in a fierce fight on the beach.

Caesar's ships were damaged by a storm, so he soon hurried back to Gaul. Next year he returned with a bigger army. He marched inland, crossed the River Thames and captured the Britons' strongest settlement. When the chiefs promised to pay money and stop helping the Gauls, Caesar sailed away.

The shield of a British warrior

Boadicea

A hundred years passed before the Romans came back. This time, they meant to conquer the island and make it part of the Roman Empire.

The Britons did not give in easily. They fought bravely under a chief named Caractacus, and, later on, there was a great rebellion led by Boadicea, Queen of the Iceni tribe. Though they burnt some of the new Roman towns, the Britons were defeated and had to accept the Romans as their rulers.

The Romans were nearly always victorious because their armies were better trained than the tribesmen. Roman soldiers wore armour and carried a short sword, two javelins and a curved shield. More important, they obeyed their officers, advanced steadily and stood firm when they were attacked.

A legionary

A centurion

A standard bearer

A Roman general

The Romans

*A Roman helmet
with a vizor-mask*

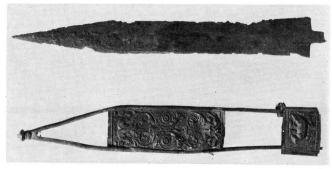

A Roman legionary's sword

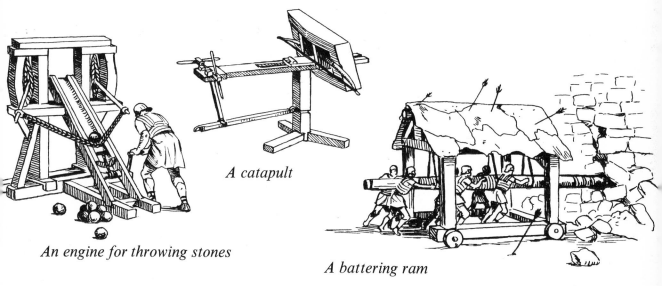

A catapult

An engine for throwing stones

A battering ram

They used archers and horsemen, as well as foot-soldiers. They were trained to march quickly and to build forts and armed camps in enemy country. When they came against a strong place defended by walls and ditches, they would bring up stone-throwing machines, battering-rams and giant catapults.

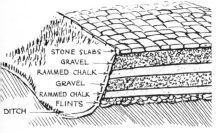

*Section through a
Roman road*

A Roman milestone

The Romans were great road-builders and as soon as they added a new province to their Empire, their officers would map out a road system.

The roads were built as straight as possible and the work was carried out by the soldiers, with prisoners to help. Layers of flints, gravel and chalk were rammed down hard and the top of the road was paved with small stone slabs.

A ditch on either side carried rain water away, and these roads were built so well that they lasted for hundreds of years.

The Romans built roads so that their legions could march quickly to any trouble spot. There were inns and forts along each route. The emperor's messengers rode along the roads with letters to the governor, and merchants also used them, though they were not allowed to hinder army traffic.

The Romans

The Romans never ruled all of Britain. They tried to conquer the fierce tribes in the north but the task was difficult and the land seemed too poor to be worth ruling. So the Emperor Hadrian ordered the soldiers to build a great wall right across the country to keep the tribesmen out.

In South Wales and along the Welsh border, army forts were built and soldiers were stationed there to control the Welsh tribes.

In southern Britain and the Midlands, life became peaceful and the Britons learned to obey their rulers. Many of the leading men began to copy Roman ways and wear Roman clothes. They sent their sons to school to learn Latin and some of them travelled to Rome itself.

The Emperor Hadrian

The guard on Hadrian's Wall

A little statue of a ploughman

In the hills and country districts, the ordinary people went on speaking the Celtic language and working in the fields as if nothing had happened. But they had to pay taxes and they were not allowed to fight other tribes, as in the old days.

When the Romans came to Britain, there were no real towns or ports, just a number of villages and settlements. As in all other parts of the Empire, they set to work to build towns.

They did this partly because they thought town-life was civilised and partly because it was much easier to make conquered people pay taxes and obey the law if they lived together in towns.

Above: the Roman theatre at St Albans. Above right: a glass cup showing a circus scene. Below: glass bowls and a jug with 'Londini' (London) scratched on it

A town street

Roman weights and measures

A Roman town was neatly laid out, with streets crossing each other in straight lines. There was an open-space for the market-place or *forum*, barracks for the soldiers, public baths, temples, law-courts, houses and shops. There was often a theatre for plays and sporting events.

The paved main streets were wide enough for a horse and cart, and stepping-stones were sometimes set at crossings so that people could cross from one pavement to the other without getting their sandals muddy.

Slaves did most of the shopping in the market but there were shops in the main street too. These were mostly small, for the house-owners would let their front room as a shop, and this was simply a counter facing the main street.

A beautiful glass vase

37

A rich man's town house often had a plain door between two of these little shops. But, once a visitor entered, he found himself in a cool courtyard with a pool or fountain in the middle. Round the courtyard were various rooms such as the library, dining-room and bedrooms. Beyond the courtyard, were the storerooms, kitchen, slaves' quarters and a garden.

Important Romans did not sit up to the table for dinner, but lay on couches, resting on one elbow to eat their food. Plates and dishes were made of fine pottery, glass and silver.

Slaves cooked the food over charcoal fires in the kitchen.

A silver dish

A strainer and a frying pan

Roman officials and some of the rich Britons built themselves country houses called villas.

These villas, mostly in southern Britain, were built of brick and timber, with a tiled or thatched roof. Buildings stood round a large courtyard, and a long covered walk or verandah ran all along the front of the rooms. This kept the rooms cool in summer and allowed people to go easily from one room to another.

A model of a great palace at Fishbourne in Sussex, as it was in 75 AD

A Roman mosaic

In the main rooms, the floors were made of tiny coloured stones set in cement. Often, the stones were arranged to make a pattern or a picture of a god's head, an animal or a fish. This kind of stone work is called *mosaic*.

The walls were plastered and painted in gay colours, sometimes with pictures of gods and goddesses. There was glass in the windows and the rooms were furnished with stools, couches and low tables.

The Romans thought that Britain was a cold foggy island and they took care to keep themselves warm in winter.

The floor of the house was supported on a number of short pillars, so there was a space underneath. A fire was lit in a stoke-hole outside and the warm air passed under the floor and up the sides of the room in hollow tiles.

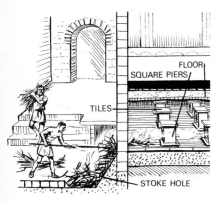

Heating under the floor of a house

A strigil or scraper and oil jug used by Roman bathers

A brooch was used for fastening the cloak

Big houses had one or more baths, because the Romans were very keen on cleanliness. There would be, first, a warm bath, then a very hot one where slaves would rub their master with sweet oil and, finally, a cold bath big enough to plunge in for a swim.

Most towns had public baths where people would go, not just to wash, but to meet their friends and talk for an hour or two. You can still see the magnificent Roman baths in the city of Bath, in Somerset.

Most men wore a short tunic, made of wool, linen or silk, with a belt round the waist. Cloaks were fastened on the right shoulder by a brooch and in winter both men and women wore hooded cloaks.

Everyone, except slaves, wore sandals, half-boots or high boots laced with thongs.

Roman shoes

The forum, or market place, was the centre of every Roman town

A comb and a hairpin

Roman magistrates, officials and rich citizens also wore the *toga*, on important occasions. This was a long piece of cloth draped round the body and thrown over the left shoulder. It was made of white wool, with a coloured band along one edge. Emperors and victorious generals wore a purple toga.

Ladies usually wore long flowing dresses. These were sleeveless with a sleeved tunic underneath. Outdoors, they would drape their big cloaks round the body and over the head.

Fashionable ladies spent a great deal of time over their hair, which was curled, waved, plaited or decked with combs. They also used make-up and plucked their eyebrows with little gold tweezers.

Children were usually taught their lessons at home. A rich man would hire a tutor or would buy a slave, possibly a Greek, who was well-educated. Rich Britons, who wanted their sons to get on in the world, would also send them to a tutor to learn arithmetic and how to speak in the law-courts.

When they were learning to write, children used a tablet of wax, marking their letters with a pencil called a *stylus*. This was a piece of wood, metal or ivory with a point at one end and a knob at the other to smooth out mistakes.

Children also learned about the gods and about their ancestors. Boys were taught boxing and sword-play, and they had to be very respectful to their parents. Girls learned sewing and how to keep house; they played with dolls and balls, and both girls and boys liked a game called knuckle-bones.

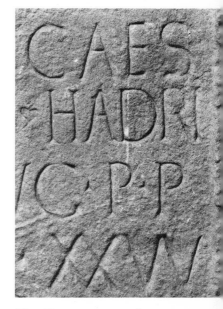

The Romans carved beautiful lettering on stone

Children played many different games

Romans and well-to-do Britons liked to go out and enjoy themselves. At the circus, they would see chariot-racing, while at Public Games in the amphitheatre, they watched contests between trained men called *gladiators*. Sometimes wild beasts were made to fight one another, or a gladiator armed with shield and sword would tackle one carrying a spear and a net.

At open-air theatres, like the one at Verulamium (St Albans), they would watch plays, dancing, wrestling, bear-baiting and cock-fights.

A gladiator's helmet

A chariot race at the circus, round an open-air oval track

Jupiter   *Christ*

The Romans had a whole family of gods. These included Jupiter, king of the gods, his wife Juno, Mars the god of war, Neptune the sea-god, Diana the huntress, and many others. There were also household gods who looked after the home.

The Romans believed in other people's gods, such as Isis of Egypt and Mithras, a Persian god, and they raised their own emperors to the level of gods.

Mithras

So, they were quite ready to add Jesus Christ to all the others, but they did not like the Christians saying there was only one God. Christianity came to Britain while the Romans ruled the island. At times, Christians were arrested and put in prison or killed, but the religion went on spreading and there were many small churches.

45

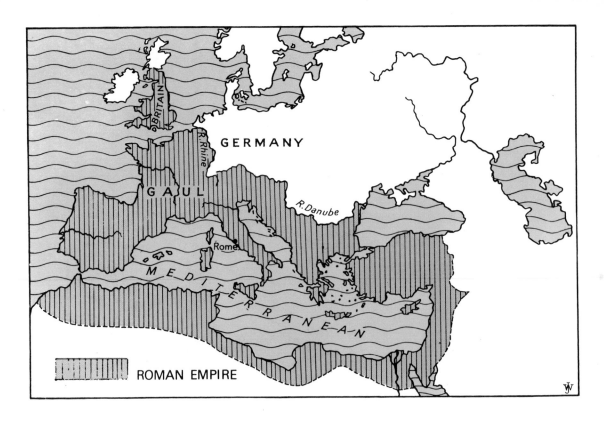

After they had ruled Britain for nearly 400 years, the Romans went away. The Empire was being attacked by fierce tribesmen called barbarians, who had defeated Roman armies and reached Italy. Rome itself was in danger and every soldier was needed at home.

The Britons were very sorry to see them go. They had no army and had not been trained to fight like soldiers. The Picts and Scots in the north had already crossed Hadrian's Wall and sea-robbers were attacking the coasts.

The British leaders sent letters to Rome, begging the Emperor to send help and not to leave them to be butchered. But it was no use. From now on, they had to defend themselves.

A Roman family

46

The Angles and Saxons 7

A Saxon ship

The Angles, Saxons and Jutes were warrior tribesmen who lived in Germany, close to the North Sea. For many years, they had been raiding Britain's coasts and the Romans built forts and a fleet to keep them at bay.

Now there was no one to stop them and they sailed along the coast of Gaul and crossed the Channel in their longships. These ships, some with a square sail but many with just fourteen pairs of oars, were ideal for attacking the east coast, where they could nose up the narrow creeks and rivers.

Saxon warriors

The Anglo-Saxons, as they were called, were tall, fair-haired warriors, armed with short one-handed swords, spears and axes. They wore armour made of metal rings sewn into a jerkin, and they carried round shields.

These sea-raiders loved fighting and were well known for their fierceness. The Saxons, who got their name from their favourite sword, called a *seax*, were said to be the cruellest fighters.

Their gods, Woden and Thor the Thunderer, were just as fierce and pitiless as the warriors themselves.

This seax blade belonged to a man called Beagnoth

Woden   Thor

47

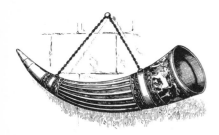

A dawn raid by the Saxons

A Saxon drinking horn

The first boatloads of attackers came simply for plunder. They would come ashore, burn the villas and towns and steal everything they could carry off. Then they would go back to their boats and sail home.

It was not long before they decided to stay. The land was better than their own; there were no Roman soldiers to drive them off and the Britons usually ran away and left their farmlands to be taken over.

Some of the Britons did fight back. Among the chiefs who won victories over the Anglo-Saxons was one called Artos or Arthur. We do not know very much about him, but he has come down in legend as King Arthur and he was supposed to have ruled a kingdom somewhere in the West Country.

Gradually, the Anglo-Saxon invaders pushed the Britons back and back, into the hills of Wales and Cornwall. They took most of the east, the south and the midlands, and they called their new country Angle-land or England.

Because they did not understand Roman ways, the Anglo-Saxons would not go and live in the looted towns. They knew nothing about building in stone and brick or about road-making, piped water, hot baths and drainage.

So the towns and the splendid villas were deserted and fell into ruins. Robbers and a few runaway slaves lived there, but everyone else forgot about town-life. The roads, however, could not be destroyed.

When they were not fighting, the Anglo-Saxons were farmers. They liked to live in a family group under their chief in a small village or settlement. This was often a clearing in the forest.

All round the settlement ran a wooden fence and a ditch to keep the herds safe at night from enemies and from the wolves in the forest.

The Roman villas fell into decay

The Anglo-Saxons cleared large areas of forest to make farms

A bucket

To build a house, they first made a frame of wood. They split two curved trees down the middle to make the end-timbers. Then they joined them by a ridge or roof-pole, added upright posts along the sides and filled in the spaces with wattle smeared with clay. When they added a thatched roof, the house looked like a barn.

The chief's house was just the same, only bigger, for he lived there with his warriors. The *hall*, as it was called, was a long, dim, smoky room, with a fire on a stone in the middle. The smoke found its way out of a hole in the roof. Windows were no more than slits, called 'eye-holes'.

The chief and his warriors lived in the hall, while the other huts were occupied by lesser men, women, children and the slaves or *serfs* who had mostly been captured in battle.

50

Inside the hall, the warriors hung their shields and weapons on the walls. The earth floor was covered in rushes, dogs roamed in and out and a valuable pair of oxen might be kept in a stall at the far end.

The Anglo-Saxons loved food and drink, and would often hold a feast. While the chief and his close friends sat at a table across the top of the hall, the warriors ranged themselves on benches on either side of the fire.

Serfs brought in great cauldrons of boiled meat, roasted joints and loaves of bread. This was the food for warriors—meat and bread, washed down by ale and mead. They drank from great goblets and curved horns, never pausing until all had gone down in one gulp.

After the feast came the singing and boasting of deeds in battle. A minstrel or gleeman would take up his harp and sing songs about the gods and great heroes.

At last, the warriors would fall asleep, wrapping themselves in their cloaks on the benches or lying on the floor near the fire. The chief and his lady went to bed in a separate hut, called a bower, where the bed was like a large box built against the wall.

A glass horn, brought to Britain from abroad

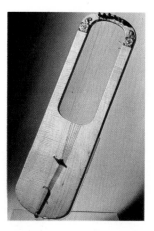

A Saxon lyre looked like this

A banquet

The lid of a purse

Clothing

Brooch

Shield

The Anglo-Saxons were good weavers and, like the Britons, they loved brightly-coloured cloth. Men wore tunics, breeches, leggings or cross-gartering, with cloaks fastened by fine brooches. The leather cross-garters were fastened to shoes which had no heels. On their heads, they wore woollen caps or rounded helmets made of leather and iron.

Shields were made of wood, covered with leather and painted. The studded rim was made of iron. Most warriors carried a spear and a throwing-axe; as a rule, only Chiefs and thanes (the leading men or nobles) carried swords.

Women wore a linen undervest and a long dress with a girdle at the waist. A sleeveless garment often went over the dress. It was shorter, to show the embroidered hem of the dress. On top came the mantle, a long piece of cloth with a hole for the head.

Indoors and outdoors, women wore the *veil*, a long piece of cloth which covered the hair completely and went down over the shoulders.

In January the farmer ploughed his land

The Anglo-Saxons lived by farming. They brought heavy ploughs with them, so they could break up the clay soils, which the earlier peoples had avoided. They grew wheat, barley, oats and rye, beans, peas and flax and they took great pride in their oxen and cattle.

The cleared land was shared out among the freemen—or *churls*—in strips, so many for each man according to his rank. The serfs had no land. Every year, one of the two or three large fields would be left to lie *fallow*, that is, to rest without any crops.

In March he dug, sowed the seed and harrowed the land

A Celtic cross on Iona. Here Christianity was not forgotten

In the districts where the Anglo-Saxons settled, one chief might become stronger than the others. Then he would be the overlord and, later on, the king. In this way, a number of small kingdoms arose, such as Kent, Essex, Wessex, Northumbria and Mercia. The kings were constantly fighting one another and, for a time, one kingdom would become greater than the others.

When the Anglo-Saxons had been in Britain for nearly 200 years, Kent was the strongest kingdom. The Pope in Rome sent a monk named Augustine to Kent to convert the king to Christianity.

King Ethelbert's wife, Queen Bertha, was already a Christian and she helped Augustine and his little band of monks and gave them a church at Canterbury. Presently, King Ethelbert became a Christian and made his people give up their heathen gods.

Two fine manuscript pictures, made in monasteries

A monk called Edwin writing a manuscript

The Britons who had been driven into the west had never forgotten the teachings of Christ they learned in Roman days. St Patrick had converted Ireland and Irish monks spread the news of Jesus in Scotland and northern England.

Gradually, nearly all of Britain became a Christian country. Churches and monasteries were built and the priests and monks taught the people to be less savage.

Monks were almost the only people who could read and write. They used quill pens and wrote on parchment, made of animal skin.

A wooden Saxon church at Greenstead in Essex

55

Children being taught in the monastery school

When the monk Bede was dying, the other monks came to his bedside and wrote down what he told them

For reading and writing, they used Latin. This was the language of educated men all over Europe. When the Pope sent a letter to a Saxon abbot or when the monks wrote down the laws for the king, they always did so in Latin. Children who were taught at the monastery school had to learn this language, too, because no-one could write in English yet.

Bede was a famous monk who lived in a monastery at Jarrow, in the north of England. He wrote many books and started a school to which boys came from France, Spain and Italy. He also wrote the first history book in England.

The Danes 8

By about the year 800, England was becoming a peaceful land. Each village had its little wooden church, the monasteries were filled with riches and the once-warlike Saxons had settled down to farming.

Suddenly, bands of fierce raiders began to attack the coasts. They were the Danes, also known as Vikings or Norsemen. They came from Denmark and Norway, where there was not enough land for farming, and they sailed across the North Sea in their dragon-ships.

A Viking ship

The Danes raid a monastery

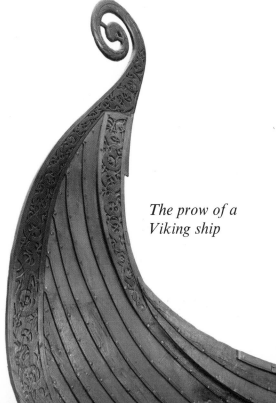

The prow of a Viking ship

A ring which belonged to King Alfred's sister, the Queen of Mercia

A jewel which belonged to King Alfred

A Danish chief and his wife

The Danelaw

Dressed in mail jerkins and iron helmets, and armed with swords, spears and two-handed battle-axes, these sea-robbers made first for the monasteries that stood near to the shore. They would seize the jewelled crosses and silver altar vessels, kill the monks and sail away. No part of the coast was safe and they even raided the Irish monasteries.

The Danes began to venture inland. They would sail up a river, leave their ships, steal horses and ride across country, killing and plundering.

In time, they seized farmland, drove out the Saxons and settled down in the eastern part of the country.

All the Saxon kingdoms had been defeated, except Wessex, in the south, and here King Alfred fought them for many years. At last, he won a great victory and forced them to make peace, but he could not drive them out altogether. So he agreed to let them live in part of the country called the Danelaw.

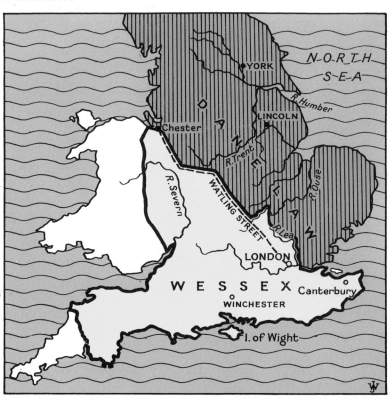

Some of the silver from a Danish hoard

Alfred the Great was a wise and brave ruler. After all the fighting, he had to build up his ruined kingdom, so he brought in some foreign monks to start the schools again; he rebuilt the churches and made the people obey the laws.

Alfred's capital was Winchester, but he repaired the Roman city of London and built a fleet of longships to stop the Danes coming to attack the kingdom.

The Danes were heathens. Their gods were Odin, Thor and Freya, and they believed that warriors who died in battle went to Valhalla, where they feasted with the gods. Alfred converted his enemy Guthrum to Christianity, and after this, many other Danes became Christians.

Viking wood carving

Danish dress and customs were similar to those of the Saxons but the Danes, besides being farmers, were much better at trading and their merchants bought and sold goods in Ireland, France and the Low Countries.

The Danes and Saxons settled down together and, under Alfred's son and grandson, Saxon England became one rich and peaceful kingdom. Then, in about 980, a new wave of raiders fell upon the country.

The head of a Viking, carved in elk horn

Edward is buried at Westminster Abbey

King Canute

A coin of Edward the Confessor

More Danes came, fiercer than ever. Whole armies roamed about, burning, slaying and seizing land. England's king, Ethelred the Unready, merely tried to buy them off with gold. Of course, they came back for more; Ethelred was driven into exile and Canute, a Dane, became King of England.

Canute ruled well. He became a Christian, made good laws and put an end to the raiding. Soon after his death, there was a Saxon king on the throne again. He was Edward the Confessor, who built an Abbey at Westminster.

In the year 1066, Harold was chosen king but he did not reign long, for William the Conqueror sailed from Normandy, defeated Harold at the Battle of Hastings and took the kingdom.

Saxon England now had many towns and villages. The towns, surrounded by a wall and ditch, were small and were mostly under the protection of some great lord or abbot.

ADWARDI:REGIS:AD:ECCLESIA PETRI

A good deal of the forest had been cut down and most people lived by farming, but there was some trading as well.

A Saxon soldier in the time of King Harold

The chief men in the country were called thanes, and the greatest of these were the earls. The earls helped the king to rule the country; they rode about with him, went hunting with him and acted as his bodyguard. When they met to give the king advice or sometimes to choose a new king, they were known as the Witan. This means a meeting of the wise men.

A meeting of the Witan

Inside a peasant's hut

Thralls at work

Below the thanes, came the freemen or *churls*, also called husbandmen. They farmed the land, along with poorer men called peasants. Each villager had so many strips of land in the big fields.

Poorest of all were the serfs or *thralls*. They had food and shelter in return for working on the land, but no wages.

Houses were still made of wood and wattle, with thatched roofs. A peasant's hut had only one room, with an earth floor and the fire on its hearth-stone. The ox, which was a man's most valuable possession, had its stall inside or alongside the hut.

The thatched wooden hall was the biggest building in the village. This was the home of the thane or lord. Here he sat down to feast with his people, seating himself with his family at the top table, where, like their forefathers, they ate huge meals, mostly of bread and meat.

Everyone liked to dress in bright colours and rich men and women fastened their cloaks with gold and silver brooches. They also wore rings, armlets and jewelled collars.

A thane and his wife

The hall was also the meeting-place, where the lord decided quarrels between villagers and punished wrong-doers.

Churches, too, were often made of wood, but some were now being built of stone. There were many monasteries in the country, though the Saxon monks had become rather lazy and were not so keen on learning and books as in the past.

An Anglo-Saxon brooch

The stone tower of a Saxon church

Index

Looking at History   R J Unstead

Book Two

The Middle Ages

Adam and Charles Black   London

Acknowledgements

Aerofilms Ltd   10
City of Bayeux   6a, b & c, 7a, b & c
Trustees of the British Museum   1, 3, 4, 14, 16b, 17a, b & d, 18a, 19a & c, 20e,
   22a, 23a–c, 24a, 24d, 25c, 26a, 27b, 30c, 32, 33a, 36b & c, 37a & b,
   38d & e, 39a, 40b, 42a, 44a & b, 46c, 47b & c, 48a & b, 50a, 51a,
   52a & c, 53b, 60a, 66b, 68a & b, 71a & b, 72a, 73a, 75a, 76a, 79b & c, 80
Country Life   48c
The Dean & Chapter of Durham Cathedral   19b
Department of the Environment   9, 43b
Mary Evans Picture Library   65a, 79a
A F Kersting   46b
London Museum   15a, 21b, 73b
Mansell Collection   16c, 24c, 25b, 30a, 45b, 49b, 55a, 77b
National Monuments Record   33c, 34a, 53a
National Portrait Gallery   49a, 77a
Crown Copyright, Public Record Office   13a, 13b, 15b, 29a
Radio Times Hulton Picture Library   5, 11, 16a, 17c, 18b, 20b, c & d,
   21, 25a, 28a, 33b, 34b & c, 46a, 47a, 52b, 58b, 61b, 62a, 64a, 65b, c & d,
   66a, 69a, 72b, 74b, cover
Trinity College, Cambridge   74a
Henry Trivick (from his book *Brasses in Gilt* published by John Baker)   2, 61a,
   69b
Victoria & Albert Museum   20a, 67a
P F White   8, 26b, 27a, 57a, 58a
Nicholas Servian, Woodmansterne Ltd   48d, 55b
Photograph 66c is reproduced by permission of Viscount De l'Isle, VC KG,
   Penshurst Place, Kent
Drawings in this book are by George Tuckwell, J C B Knight, Mary Houston,
   Iris Brooke and others.
Designed by Karen Bowen

Published by A & C Black (Publishers) Ltd
35 Bedford Row London WC1R 4JH

ISBN 0 7136 1421 8 limp
     0 7136 1417 X net

First published in this edition 1974. Reprinted 1975, 1977, 1978 & 1979
© 1974 A & C Black Ltd
Previous editions © 1953, 1961 A & C Black Ltd

Printed in Great Britain by Sir Joseph Causton & Sons Ltd,
London and Eastleigh

Contents

Giving a child a ride in a wheelbarrow

This book is about the life of ordinary people in the Middle Ages. It tells you how they built and furnished their homes, how they lived, worked and enjoyed themselves; you will read about their clothes, food, games and punishments.

You will not find very much about kings, queens and battles in this book, but to help you to know who were the rulers, and what were the chief events in the Middle Ages, there are three very short chapters called 'Happenings.' The full stories of these happenings and of the many famous men and women can be found in other history books, but this is a book about everyday people and things.

The Normans 1

The last big invasion of Britain was made by the Normans, from France, led by Duke William of Normandy.

William declared that Edward the Confessor had promised him the crown of England, but as Harold would not give up his kingdom, William and the Normans made ready to attack.

They built ships and filled them with stores, horses and even parts of wooden forts, which were to be put together when they had landed.

In 1066 the Normans landed in Sussex, with an army of mounted knights and foot-soldiers. They defeated Harold and the Saxons in a great battle—the Battle of Hastings. Harold and most of the Saxon nobles were killed, and William the Conqueror became King of England.

The Bayeux Tapestry, which was embroidered on a long strip of linen, tells the story of the invasion. On the next two pages are some pictures from it.

Saxon soldiers at Hastings

Duke William's ships approaching England

Here the Normans are cutting down trees and building their ships.

The Normans go on board their ships.

The Normans sail. (Can you see their horses in the ships?)

They land near Hastings.

The battle is very fierce.

At last the Normans win and the Saxons run away.

A Norman knight and his lady

Actors dressed as knights at a modern tournament

The Normans who came with William spoke French and dressed like the man and woman on the left.

The knight's helmet had a nose-piece. His coat of mail was called a hauberk. It was a leather jacket with iron rings sewn on to it. At the bottom there was a slit so that he could ride comfortably on horseback. His cloth stockings had leather cross-garters.

The Normans carried swords, battle-axes and lances. Unlike the Saxons, they had a force of archers and the knights charged on horseback.

The lady wore her hair in plaits, sometimes with a veil over it. She wore two tunics (or frocks) with a jewelled belt. Her cloak was fastened with a cord.

Dover Castle. The square keep and the towered inner bailey were built by Henry II

Norman castles

The Saxons hated the Normans, but as they had lost their leaders in the battle, they could not fight on. William was afraid that they might give trouble, so he built castles outside the Saxon towns. In each castle there were Norman soldiers ready to stop the Saxons raising an army.

The first castles had to be built quickly. Each castle was just a wooden tower on a hill, or mound of earth, with a fence round it and a ditch outside.

In time, the wooden towers were replaced by great stone castles. William only built two stone castles —the Tower of London and Colchester Castle.

During the reigns of later Norman kings, many stone castles were built in different parts of the country.

William's early castles were just wooden towers built on a hill

9

Berkhamsted Castle. The mound and the bailey are easily seen

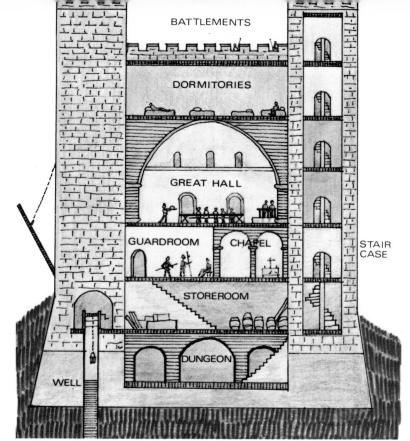

BATTLEMENTS

DORMITORIES

GREAT HALL

GUARDROOM   CHAPEL

STAIR CASE

STOREROOM

DUNGEON

WELL

The keep

A gateway with a portcullis

To enter the castle, the Normans crossed over the moat by the drawbridge (which the soldiers could wind up and down from the gatehouse) and went through a great gateway, with thick wooden gates. The gateway also had a portcullis, a strong, pointed iron fence which was drawn upwards to allow people to pass through. When an enemy approached, it was quickly lowered.

Inside the high walls was a big yard called the *outer bailey*. Against the walls were stables and sheds for corn and hay. Cows and sheep were driven into the outer bailey for safety, in troubled times.

The *inner bailey* was a smaller yard, reached by crossing another drawbridge. Here was the Great Tower or *keep*, with walls six metres thick.

10

At the top of the keep were the battlements, where soldiers kept a look-out over the countryside to see what the Saxons were doing.

Below the battlements were the sleeping-rooms for the lord and his important visitors. Other people slept on benches in the *Great Hall* or lay down on the floor wrapped in their cloaks.

A dungeon

The Great Hall was a long, bare room with small windows in the thick walls. The floor was made of rough oak planks and was covered with rushes. The fire was on a stone slab in the middle, and the smoke had to find its way out through the little windows.

On the next floor were the guard-room and the chapel.

At the very bottom of the keep were store-rooms for food and armour. The well might be here, and also a dungeon for prisoners.

Norman builders at work

The Great Hall of a Norman castle

The staircases were cut in the thickness of the walls and had narrow, stone steps.

There was very little furniture: long tables, which could be taken down to clear a space, benches and two or three chests for clothes and armour. At one end the floor was raised. Here the lord and lady had their meals. The rest of the family and the knights sat lower down.

The binding of Domesday Book. The book has been looked after with great care over the centuries

Domesday Book

William wanted to learn all about his new kingdom and how much it was worth, so he sent his men to find out about every town, village, farm and field in all the land: how big they were, who owned them and how much tax they could pay.

Notes on every place in the country were written down in the Domesday Book. They were written in Latin, in red and black ink. The great book was finished in 1086. It can still be seen in London. The binding in the photograph above was made in Tudor times.

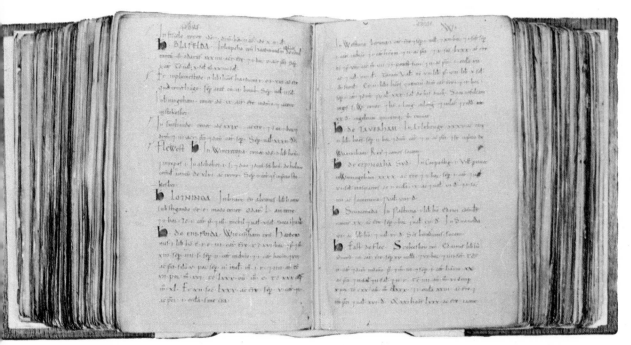

Norman houses

William lent castles to the barons, but he did not like them to build castles for themselves. Some Norman knights were given land and they built stone manor-houses. A manor means an estate, with one or more villages and all the land round about.

Each manor-house had a wall built round it, so that it was like a small castle. The hall, or living-room, was upstairs, for safety. It was reached by a stone staircase outside the house. The windows were bigger than the slits found in castles. They had no glass yet. Wooden shutters kept out the rain and the wind.

Downstairs, as in the castles, there were store-rooms and space for the serving men.

Getting out of a coat of mail

A fortified manor house

By drawing a curtain or screen across one end of the hall, the lord made a small room for himself and his lady. This private room was called the *solar*. They would go there to talk and the lady would sew. They also slept there. Sometimes the solar was an upper room, reached by a ladder, or by an outside staircase.

The lord had a big wooden bed, with a feather mattress, a bolster, linen sheets and a coverlet of fur. As they had no cupboards, the lord and lady hung their clothes on a pole sticking out from the wall. Jewels, money and important manuscripts were kept in a heavy chest. The lord also had a little room cut in the thickness of the walls, called the *treasury*. He kept his wine and other valuables in there.

Stools and the baby's cradle made up the rest of the furniture, and there was a fireplace against one of the outer walls.

There was often a pet hawk in the solar, or a squirrel in a cage. Hunting dogs were kept at every manor-house.

A bronze water jug

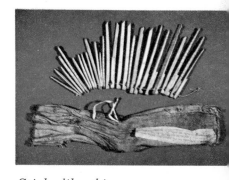

Sticks like this, called tallies were used to record payments. They were kept in the treasury

15

A baker's oven

The kitchen was a separate building, across the yard, so the food was not very hot by the time it reached the hall. Later on, the lord made a covered way from his kitchen, and later still, the kitchen became part of the house.

In the kitchen

The lord liked good food and he had cooks and scullions to prepare it.

At this time a lot of meat was eaten: beef, mutton, pork and venison (deer), and all kinds of birds and fish, especially herrings and eels. Poor people lived mainly on vegetables: peas, beans and cabbages, with a piece of bacon now and then.

Eating a picnic during a hunt

The kitchen of a manor house prepared food for many people

16

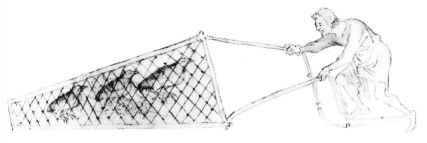

Trapping birds

Hawking

There was never enough hay for all the cattle in winter, so most of them were killed in the autumn. The meat was then put into barrels of salt water to save it from going bad. Everyone soon grew tired of eating salt meat and herrings, and they added spices to make their food more tasty.

The lord and his knights would go hunting and hawking to get fresh meat. Roast chickens, geese and swans were popular dishes, and even peacocks were served if the king came on a visit.

There were other huts in the manor-yard besides the kitchen. There was the brew-house, where the ale and mead were made, the pantry, the dairy and the buttery. As there were no shops, nearly everything was made at the manor-house.

Milking

Trapping rabbits with a ferret

The lord at his table

A jester

The lord had his dinner at 10 o'clock in the morning and his supper about 6 o'clock.

His table stood higher than the rest. In the centre it had a large salt-cellar. Ordinary people sat lower down in the hall, 'below the salt.'

At the lord's table there was French wine to drink, as well as ale. Glasses and goblets were now used for drinking. There were plates, knives and spoons, but no forks.

A page from another noble family waited on the lord and his guests. Before and after dinner, he brought them a bowl of water and a napkin, so that they could wash their hands.

After dinner, the minstrels played and sang, and the jester made everyone laugh.

18

How the people lived

The king was the ruler of the kingdom. He owned the land and forests. He gave land to the barons and to the abbots, who knelt down and, placing their hands in his, promised to be his men, to obey his laws and to give him soldiers and money when they were needed. Thus, the Normans said that every man had an overlord.

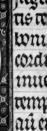

Barons, knights and abbots were the lords of the manor. They kept some land for themselves and gave the rest to the villeins (or peasants).

Every villein also did homage to his lord. This means that he promised to be his man and to obey the customs of the manor. He also promised, in return for some land, to work on the lord's land and to give him various things.

Doing homage

Using a harrow on the land

Sowing seed in October

Storing corn

A villein in Norman times might have to do these things:

Plough 4 acres (about $1\frac{1}{2}$ hectares) for his lord in the spring. Lend him 2 oxen for 7 days a year. Work 3 days a week on his domain (land). Pay 1 hen and 16 eggs each year. Bring 1 cartload of wood from the forest to the manor-house. Grind his corn in the lord's mill. Pay a fine if his daughter married. Pay a fine if he sent his son to school at the monastery.

He could never leave the village except to carry a message or to go with his lord to war.

On some manors the customs and payments were a little different. But, generally, a man who held a lot of land had to do more work for the lord and make more payment than a villein who only held a little land.

Early mills were all watermills

Sickles and pruning knives

Planting trees and working the land

All this was written down in the Court Roll and the lord's *steward* and the village *reeve* saw that it was carried out. Any villein who disobeyed was brought to the Manor Court to pay a fine.

A villein who was able to save enough money, liked to pay a rent for his land instead of doing 'week-work' for the lord. Then he could spend all his time on his own land. He was now a freeman, and no longer a serf.

If the lord was cruel, or if a villein had committed a crime, he might run away to the forest and become an outlaw. Everyone was supposed to arrest or kill an outlaw, but if he could reach a town and not be caught for a year and a day, he became a freeman.

A villein's cott or hut

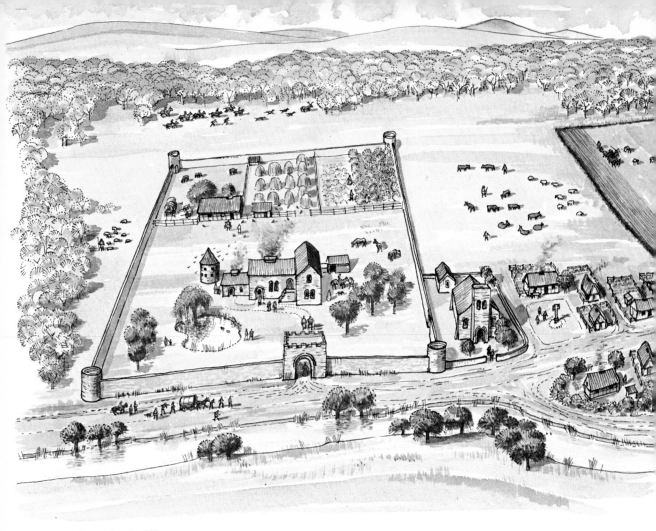

A typical village

Storing the harvest

In the village, besides the stone manor-house, there were the church and the cross, the priest's house and twenty or thirty huts for the villeins. These were made of wattle and daub (wicker and mud) with thatched roofs. The smoky little huts had a fire in the middle of their one room.

Most manors had three large fields, one growing wheat, one barley and one resting (lying fallow). In the wheat and barley fields there would also be some oats, rye, beans and peas. Each field was shared out into strips of land, with little grass paths between. This meant that everyone had a share of good and bad land.

Working on the manor

The corn was taken to the lord's mill to be ground into flour. The villeins had to pay for this.

Bringing corn to the mill

Outside the fields was the common-land, where the animals could graze. Each one was marked with its owner's mark. If a cow strayed, it was put in a little yard with a fence round it, called the pound. The owner had to pay two pence to get it back.

Down by the river was the meadow-land, where the long grass was cut and dried to provide hay in winter.

Ploughing with oxen

The women worked hard, making butter and looking after the little gardens of peas, beans and cabbages. (There were no potatoes yet.) In the evenings they spun sheep's wool into thread and wove it into rough cloth.

Children looked after the animals and scared birds from the crops.

It was a very hard life for the villeins, who grumbled continuously about their tasks, especially at haymaking and harvest, when they had to do extra work for the lord. The reeve was allowed to beat them if they did not work hard.

The way in which people lived on the manor is called the *Feudal System*.

At Christmas people dressed up as mummers

Holy Days

The villagers enjoyed many Holy Days, such as Christmas Day, May-day and Midsummer Eve. The villeins went to church on these days, and afterwards sports and dancing were held on the green, with races, wrestling, jumping, archery and throwing lances. People danced round the maypole and afterwards went to the ale house and made merry.

At Christmas everyone went to the manor-house for a feast in the hall. There were rough games afterwards, like *hoodman blind*.

Dancing round the maypole

Wrestling

25

2 Happenings

William I was the first Norman king. He was strong and wise, and he made the barons obey him. He could be cruel, and when the Saxons in the north rebelled, he punished them with fire and death, but when people obeyed him, William treated them fairly.

Hereward the Wake was the leader of a Saxon rebellion. With a company of other rebels he hid in the marshes of Ely, but although William's soldiers found his hiding-place, he escaped.

William Rufus, the Red-Head, was the next king. He was killed by an arrow when hunting.

Henry I, his brother, kept peace and order in the land. Trade was good. Many churches and monasteries were built and towns grew larger. The Normans and Saxons were now learning to live together in peace.

When Henry I died the nobles would not have his daughter, Matilda, as queen. Stephen, her cousin, was made king instead. Then there was a civil war between the barons, and people went in fear of their lives.

The barons built castles for themselves and would not obey the king. Many cruel things were done and men said, 'God and his Saints slept.'

Orford Castle, built by Henry II

Henry II (1154) was a strong king. He made the barons obey him and pulled down some of the castles they had built without royal permission.

He also tried to force the clergy, who were very powerful, to obey his rules. Thomas à Becket, Archbishop of Canterbury, would not do so and for a long time he argued with the king.

Henry, in a fit of temper, caused some of his knights to kill Becket in Canterbury Cathedral, but he was sorry for this deed and did penance by walking through the city and by being whipped in the Cathedral.

People called Becket Saint Thomas and went as pilgrims to Canterbury, to pray at his tomb.

A small Norman church

Henry II and Becket

The murder of Becket

27

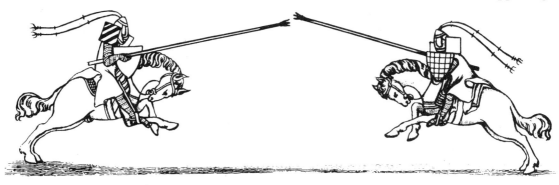

Jousting

The barons loved fighting and often had tournaments for sport in their castle-yards. So, when Richard I, the Lion-Heart, took an army to the Holy Land for the Third Crusade, they followed him eagerly.

For 200 years, French, German, and English knights went on Crusades. They captured Jerusalem from the Turks and ruled most of the Holy Land for a time. But they were always quarrelling among themselves.

Saladin, a great leader, recaptured Jerusalem in 1187 and although Richard I defeated Saladin, he could not win Jerusalem back.

A siege

When they came home, the Crusaders brought back new ideas about building, warfare and castles. They also brought carpets, sugar, and fruits such as lemons. In the East, they had learned about stars, medicine and mathematics.

King John quarrelled with the barons and the clergy. The Pope said that he must be turned off the throne but John made his peace and continued to do as he pleased. In 1215, the barons forced him to put his seal to Magna Carta, a charter or list of their rights. His promise to rule well was soon broken.

Robin Hood and his Merry Men are said to have lived at this time in Sherwood Forest. They were outlaws who had run away from their lords. Robin Hood was a popular hero, for he robbed the rich to help the poor.

There were also many bands of robbers who hid in the forests and robbed travellers.

Magna Carta

Robin Hood

A crusader ship

29

3 The Middle Ages

A bishop

By this time the Normans had settled down with the Saxons and had become the English people.

The monasteries

Although there was much fighting and cruelty, people were very religious. The bishops and abbots were as powerful as the barons. They owned numerous manors, because when rich men died, they left money and land to the monasteries, asking the monks to pray for their souls.

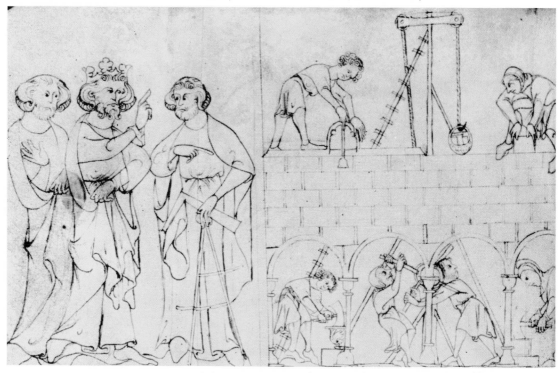

Building the abbey of St Albans

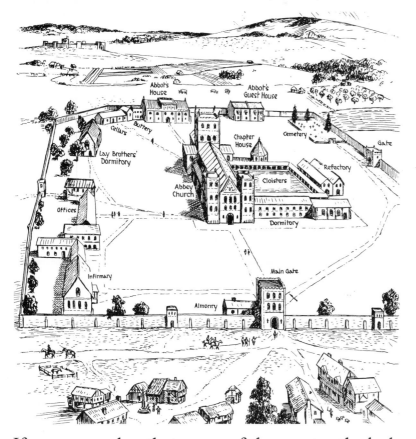

Feeding the poor

If you remember that many of the great cathedrals were once the monastery churches, then you can guess how big an abbey was, for there were many other buildings as well: the almonry, where money and food were given to the poor; the cloisters, where the monks could walk up and down in all weathers, and where they taught the young monks; and the infirmary, where the monks looked after sick people.

In the refectory (dining-room) of a large abbey, scores of monks and visitors could sit down to dinner at one time.

There were many monasteries in different parts of the country, each in the charge of an abbot or a prior who was lord over towns and villages in the neighbourhood.

Looking after the sick

31

Fishing

The Monks were:

the Abbot

the Prior (his chief helper)

the Sub-Prior (his second helper)

the Sacristan, who looked after the church

the Hospitaller, who looked after visitors

the Infirmarian, who looked after the sick

the Almoner, who helped the poor

the ordinary monks, who obeyed these chief monks, and also did gardening, farming, fishing and building, as well as praying and singing hymns in Latin.

In some monasteries, there were also lay-brothers who were chosen to help with the farm work. They lived at the abbey but did not spend as much time in church as the *choir monks*.

Lastly, there were the novices, who were boys learning to be monks.

Building

A new monk has his head shaved; this is called a tonsure

Praying together was an important part of religious life

The cellarer looked after the food and drink – but sometimes he helped himself

The monasteries did much good work: they looked after sick people, for there were no hospitals in these days; they helped the poor, gave shelter to travellers, and taught reading and writing.

Many churches were built by the monks in Norman times. They built for the glory of God. Their work took many, many years to finish and much of it can still be seen in our cathedrals.

On the right is Durham Cathedral. Notice the Norman arches, which are rounded at the top, and the decorated columns.

Durham Cathedral

33

A monk's day

Long before daylight, all the monks went down to the great church to say prayers called Matins. The next service, Lauds, lasted until 2 or 3 o'clock.

The monks went back to bed until daybreak; then came a service called Prime, followed by a light breakfast of bread with wine or ale.

At 8 o'clock in the Chapter House, the abbot told the monks their duties for the day and any who had misbehaved were punished.

After Chapter they walked awhile in the cloisters.

At 10 o'clock came the most important service, High Mass, followed by dinner in the Refectory, when the monks did not speak but were read to from the Bible or a holy book.

After dinner came the work of the day—gardening, farming, writing, building or fishing.

Evening prayers called Vespers were said before supper and at 7 or 8 o'clock came the last service, Compline, after which the monks went to bed.

Soon after midnight, the bell rang for the next day to begin.

The Chapter house at Salisbury

Writing a manuscript

A service

Friars

There were also friars, who wandered from place to place, preaching and helping the poor: Black Friars, White Friars, and best loved, the Grey Friars who tried, like St. Francis, to be kind and gentle. They looked after the sick and became famous for their skill and knowledge in curing illness.

There were also nuns, who lived together in religious houses called nunneries. They led much the same kind of lives as the monks, attending church services, teaching children and doing needlework.

John Wycliffe was a famous preacher, who tried to make men lead better lives. His followers, called Lollards, used to preach on the village green, or by the town cross.

A Lollard preaching

The friars went from village to village

35

A company of pilgrims at supper at an inn

A lady sometimes rode behind a man

Pilgrims and travellers

Everyone tried to go on a pilgrimage, to say prayers at a holy place, at least once in his life. Pilgrims went to Canterbury, St. Albans, Glastonbury and other holy places as far away as Spain, Rome and the Holy Land. A party of people would set off together. It made a holiday for them.

Pilgrims usually walked on their long journeys. A pilgrim might wear a cockle-shell in his hat to show that he had been to Compostella in Spain. He was often called a palmer, because he carried a piece of palm from the Holy Land.

A coach, drawn by five horses

Carts were used to take criminals to execution

A small carriage

Noble ladies rode in a clumsy coach pulled by five or six horses, or they were carried by servants in a litter. Rich travellers rode on horseback, and ladies on a pillion seat behind a servant. It was disgraceful to ride in a cart, because that was how prisoners were taken to be executed.

Merchants took their goods from town to town on pack-horses or mules.

The roads were very bad indeed because no one mended them. They were only rough tracks. Sometimes a farmer was fined for ploughing up the King's Highway.

Packhorses

The Wife of Bath, a nun and the nuns' priest, from Chaucer's Canterbury Tales

Geoffrey Chaucer wrote down the stories which some pilgrims told on the way to St. Thomas à Becket's tomb. They are called *The Canterbury Tales*.

Journeys were slow and dangerous, because of robbers. Travellers stayed the night at inns, which had a bunch of holly outside for a sign. It took two or three days to go from London to Canterbury.

Geoffrey Chaucer

Pilgrims used seals like this to show that they had been on pilgrimage

Obeying the law

There were no law courts yet. A man was punished at the Manor Court by his lord, who would make him pay a fine for such crimes as letting his beasts wander in the corn, or for taking firewood. He could also be tried at the Shire Moot by the Sheriff.

There were some old Saxons customs still in use.

A savage medieval punishment

If a man was accused of a crime, he might suffer *ordeal by fire*. He had to carry a piece of red-hot iron for three paces. His hand was then bound up. If, when it was undone three days later, there were no blisters, he was innocent, but if he had blisters he was punished or killed.

Ordeal by water meant that he was tied up and thrown into the river. If he floated he was guilty of the crime.

Ordeal by fire

Trial by combat

Ordeal by combat was introduced by the Normans. A noble had to fight the man who accused him. Both men had shields and special axes; they might fight all day until one cried 'Craven'—then he was put to death. Sometimes a noble got a champion to fight for him.

Henry II made new laws and stopped most of these cruel ways of trial. He ordered *trial by jury*. This meant that twelve good men came to swear what they knew about the man who was accused.

As there were no police, the king's laws were often broken, and if the king was weak, the barons did as they liked. Men sometimes bribed others to say things which were not true.

At this time there were many strange punishments. Cheats and thieves were put in the pillory, or had to sit all day in the stocks, so that everyone laughed at them and pelted them with rubbish.

A friar and a woman in the stocks

A fishmonger who sold bad fish

A baker who made poor bread would be dragged on a sledge, with a loaf tied to his neck.

If a fishmonger sold bad fish, he would be taken round the town with stinking fish hanging from his neck.

A priest being punished

Sometimes a man's hair was cut off and he was marched to prison with 'minstrelsy' (music and drums). A bad priest would have to ride through the streets sitting facing his horse's tail and wearing a paper crown.

A woman who nagged her husband was called a 'scold'. She was tied on a chair and dipped in the river. This chair was called the *ducking stool*.

She might also have to wear a *scold's bridle,* which had a piece of iron to go in the mouth to keep her tongue down.

The ducking stool

41

*A nobleman
beheaded in public*

There was no torture in England at this time, but sometimes ears or hands were cut off and noses slit for punishment. Rogues were whipped and murderers hanged in public for everybody to see, but nobles could choose to be beheaded.

In the towns, the mayor and aldermen were supposed to keep order, and they paid the *common sergeant* and the *watchman* to do the work for them.

After curfew (which means 'cover fire' and was a law made by the Normans to make the Saxons go to bed early), no one was allowed to be out on the streets, or the watchman would arrest them. Curfew was at 8 o'clock in the winter and 9 o'clock in the summer.

More Happenings 4

Simon de Montfort

King John died whilst at war with the barons and his nine-year-old son became Henry III. When he grew up, Henry ruled badly and offended the barons. They were led by Simon de Montfort, who called the first Parliament in 1265. It was a meeting of knights, barons and citizens from some of the towns.

Edward I came next. He was a strong king who restored order. He conquered Wales, for the Welsh people had never obeyed the Normans, and he built some fine castles like Harlech, which can still be seen today.

He also tried to conquer the Scots, but he did not succeed. He was called Edward Long-shanks, Hammer of the Scots.

Harlech Castle, built by Edward I

A battle, about the year 1350

Edward II was a weak king, and the Scots, led by Robert Bruce, defeated the English at the Battle of Bannockburn.

Then came Edward III, who spent much of his time fighting the French. His son was the Black Prince. The English army led by the King or Prince, was made up of knights or nobles, with their squires and pages, and the foot-soldiers, who were villeins, armed with longbows.

A page was a noble's son, who at the age of seven was sent to live at another castle, to wait at table and to learn manners. When he was fourteen, he became a squire and learnt to fight and to help his knight with his armour. One day, if he proved brave in battle, he would win his spurs and become a knight.

Sir Geoffrey Luttrell of Lincolnshire setting off for war

44

The nobles were fond of melées and jousts, which were held at court. Two knights, separated by a low fence, charged each other at top speed, each trying to unseat the other with his lance.

The English longbow could kill a man in armour nearly 200 metres away. The bow was as long as the archer. It was made of yew and the bowstring of hemp or flax. The arrow was a *cloth-yard* (just under a metre) long and was made of ash with grey goose feathers. The archer wore a bracer or laced leather sleeve on his left arm.

The French used crossbows, which were more powerful than longbows, but as they had to be wound up, they could not be fired as quickly.

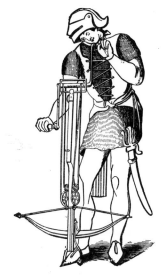

A crossbowman

A tournament

An army on the march

Practising archery

The villeins, who followed their lords to battle, carried longbows. They were good archers, because Edward made a law that all men must practise archery at the butts in the village church-yards, instead of playing football.

Towns and castles were so strong that a siege lasted a long time, and if the attackers could not batter a hole in the walls, they surrounded it and starved the people inside. This was how Edward III captured Calais.

Sieges could also be dangerous for the attackers, because of a disease known as *camp fever*. Both the Black Prince and Henry V died of illnesses caused by unhealthy conditions in camp.

Edward III

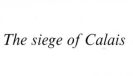

The siege of Calais

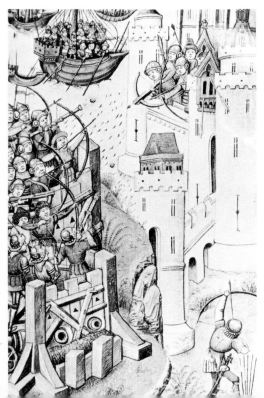

Tending sheep

A sheep-pen

During the French Wars a terrible disease came from the East called the Black Death (1348). Thousands of people died and some villages and manors had hardly anyone left alive.

There were not enough men to plough the land and sow the corn, so the lords of the manor let grass grow instead. They kept many sheep on it, because their wool was valuable.

Sheep are loaded on board ship to be sold abroad

Spinning wool and dyeing cloth

English wool was very good and much of it was sold to Flanders (Belgium). Weavers from Flanders came to live in England and wool towns in Norfolk, Suffolk and Gloucestershire became very rich. Merchants built fine houses and churches.

When so many sheep were kept, a large number of villeins lost their strips of land. They became poor and unhappy and said 'Sheep eat men.'

A merchant's house in Essex

Church at Lavenham, a wool town in Suffolk

The Black Prince was never king. He died, worn out with much fighting, and his son, Richard II, was only a boy when he became king.

After the Black Death, the villeins grumbled because there were new laws which forced them to stay with their lord and work much harder. This was necessary because so many people had died. They also had to pay heavy taxes, and at this they rebelled. Led by Wat Tyler and John Ball, a poor preacher, they marched angrily to London. This was the Peasants' Revolt.

Richard II

In this old picture, the young king, Richard II, is promising to help the peasants, but these promises were not kept. Later on the nobles rebelled against him and they made his cousin king in his place, as Henry IV.

In 'Happenings' you have read a lot about the kings. This is because the king was the real ruler of England in the Middle Ages. If he was weak, or a boy-king, he could not keep the barons in order and their quarrels and private wars made life wretched and dangerous for everybody.

Richard II going to meet the peasants. His promises to them were not kept

5 Town Life in the Middle Ages

*A street in a
medieval town*

After the Normans came, towns grew bigger, especially London, which was now the capital of England. Even so, they were not very large towns, for there were fewer people in all England than there are in London today. The streets were narrow and the houses were built close together.

Round each town there was a thick wall, for safety against enemies, and the town gates were locked every night at sunset.

*London about 1430,
showing the Tower
and London Bridge*

The townsfolk were freemen who had paid their lord a sum of money to be free and they had to look after themselves. They chose a mayor, who, with the help of his aldermen, ruled the town. Every town had its own laws and punishments. The mayor told the people what they must do through the town crier, who called out messages and news at the market cross.

A town crier

Shops

There were shops in the town, but they were not large buildings with glass windows. When a man had things to sell—shoes or cloth, candles or pewter cups—he put them on a stall in the front of his downstairs room and went on working at his trade. People who did not live in the town often sold their wares outside its walls.

In this picture an artist of the Middle Ages has tried to show town life of his time. Notice the stalls outside the walls, the changing of foreign money in the gateway, the style of clothes and the artist's way of showing a scene inside a house

51

Blacksmiths at work

A baker and his wife

Some towns, especially in Italy and Flanders, were like little states. They had their own laws, taxes, and trading rights. For a sum of money, the townsmen might get a charter from the king; then they could have a mayor and a market.

Shopkeepers nearly always sold the goods which they made themselves, and the men who made one kind of thing lived in the same street. There were streets called Candlemakers' Row, Butchers' Row, Glovers' Row, Ironmongers' Lane, Milk Street, Silver Street and Honey Lane.

They hung the sign of their trade outside their shop—a fish, a boot or a pair of scissors. Some of these old signs can still be found occasionally. Names were not written over the shops because few people could read.

A town bridge

A medieval shop

A prosperous merchant

Gilds

The craftsmen joined together in gilds (or guilds), which were meetings of men in the same trade. There were the Tailors' Gild, the Goldsmiths' Gild and many others.

These gilds did good work. They made sure that their members charged honest prices and used good materials.

They helped widows and orphans, and it is known that the Carpenters' Gild gave fourteen pence a week to a member who was ill.

The gilds also helped to look after the town church and to pay money for candles on the altar, for building a new chapel or for a school. Sometimes they gave money to mend the town bridge.

The Gildhall at Thaxted in Essex

A man had to prove his skill before being allowed to join a gild

53

*Football in the
streets was a rough
game*

When a boy was about fourteen, he might become
an apprentice, which means that he would learn a
trade for seven years. He went to live with his
master, to learn how to make clothes, or armour,
or whatever his master made. At night he slept in
the shop. He would also help to sell the goods,
crying out to passers-by, 'What d'ye lack? What
d'ye lack?'

The apprentice boys were full of fun and liked to
play football, handball, marbles and tops, but
their masters would beat them if they dodged
their work. They also liked archery and the cruel
sport of bull-baiting, in which fierce dogs were set
to attack a bull.

Streets in the town

Every town had many churches, some of them built with money given by rich merchants. Arches and doorways were now more pointed than those built by the Normans. People were religious and no one missed going to church on Sundays and holy days.

In the middle of the town was the market-place and the town cross, where the king's herald or the town crier called out the news, and friars or Lollards preached. Here, too, were the stocks and the pillory.

The narrow streets were very dirty. There were cobbles outside the shops, but in the middle of the road was a kind of gutter into which everyone threw their rubbish, even sweepings from the stables, dead dogs and other smelly things.

A worker in a mint. Coins were minted in many towns in Britain

A cathedral door

Salisbury Cathedral

The mayor was always trying to get the streets cleaner. He would punish butchers for killing animals outside their shops and for throwing down the parts which no one could eat.

People threw dirty water from upstairs windows, and pigs and chickens wandered in and out of the rubbish looking for food.

Pigs were a great nuisance and some people even made pig-sties in the streets and alleys, until a law was made which said 'He who shall wish to feed a pig, must feed it in his house.' Any pig found wandering could be killed though the owner could pay a fine to get it back

Medieval buildings in Warwick. Beneath the gild chapel, you can see the town gate

The townsfolk did not like carts with iron wheels, because they broke up the paving stones, so sledges were often used instead.

Travelling merchants had to pay a toll before they could come inside the town gates. It cost more for a big cart loaded with mill-stones, than for a small cart which would damage the road less.

Water had to be fetched from the river or drawn from wells in the town. It could also be bought from water-carriers, who took it round the streets in carts or buckets.

A water carrier

For a long time castles and monasteries had had lead water-pipes. Now they were laid in some streets. People used to cut the pipes to get water for themselves, which made the mayor angry.

As the houses were very close together and made partly of wood, everyone was frightened of fire. Outside some of the houses hung leather fire buckets and big hooks for pulling off burning thatch.

Fire hook and leather bucket

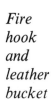

A carved wooden head on a medieval house

Houses were of many different shapes and sizes, because people built houses just as they pleased. Land was scarce inside the small walled towns, so if a merchant wanted to make his house bigger, he added another storey on top.

In these days there were lepers, people who had a terrible disease called leprosy, which, it is thought, the Crusaders brought back from the East. They were not allowed to live in the towns. Food was left for them outside the town walls and kind people gave money to build special houses for them to live in. Lepers carried a bell to warn passers-by and cried out 'Unclean, unclean.'

There were also many beggars wandering from town to town. They were rough, wild men who often robbed people to get food and clothing.

Doctors had no cure for leprosy

Beggars

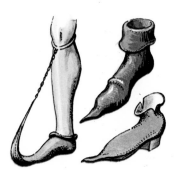

Clothes

Nobles

The dress of the nobles in the Middle Ages became very gay and brightly coloured. The courtiers wore long gowns with wide sleeves, which touched the ground, or short pleated top-coats, belted and edged with fur. They pulled their waists in tightly and padded their chests.

They wore stockings, often with different coloured legs, and shoes so pointed that sometimes the points were curled up and, fastened to a garter below the knee, by a silver chain. Men wore hats both indoors and out. They would keep their hats on when eating their dinner.

Ladies of the Court

The ladies wore tall pointed hats made of gold and silver tissue, with a velvet or fur roll round them and a large veil. Some hats were made with two horns; others were jewelled. Dresses were long and full and the under-dress (the cotte) hardly showed at all; it was becoming a petticoat.

Merchants

Merchants and their wives usually wore long dark gowns because they were not allowed to dress in such bright colours as the nobles.

Apprentices

Apprentices were forbidden to wear fine clothes or to try to copy the upper classes.

A merchant and his wife

Children

Children were dressed like grown-ups. A noble boy's long boots would be made of soft leather. Small children wore nothing but a tunic in summer.

Knights

For jousting, knights wore their full armour and sometimes a coloured surcoat on top. Their helmets were often topped by a crest—a bird or animal made of wood and leather.

The poor folk

These still wore rough belted tunics, leggings and wooden clogs, or shoes of thick cloth. Peasant women wore long dresses of coarse cloth and hoods or wimples on their heads. The children had short tunics and were bare-footed.

Nearly all men at this time wore a useful garment called a capuchon, which was a hood with a short cape. Later on, the merchants twisted it up on their heads like a turban. Both men and women wore cloaks

A brass rubbing showing a knight and his lady. Notice how his hair was cut as a padding under the helmet

The clothing of the poor

Ladies out hunting

Nobles carried daggers, and pouches at their belts (instead of pockets) and sometimes a little whip for beating servants. The ladies had handbags.

Shoes were narrow and pointed, but heels were not yet in use.

Clothes were mostly made of woollen cloth, some of it very fine, and linen. Noble ladies bought silk from Italy and heavy material called damask, which originally came from Damascus. Fur was very popular for linings and trimmings.

Fairs

Great fairs were held (especially at Northampton and Winchester) to which traders from all parts, even from across the sea, came to bring their goods. Such a fair as St. Giles's Fair at Winchester would last for sixteen days. The fairground was just outside the walls, in a big field.

At the fair there would be nobles and poor men, beggars and thieves, travellers from foreign lands and merchants arriving with pack-horses.

All kinds of goods were on sale: leather, wine, bales of wool, beautiful glasses from Italy and mirrors from France, spices from the East, carpets and oranges, silks and velvets for the rich people and parchment for the monks to write on.

There were other fine sights to see: jugglers balancing swords and swallowing fire, mummers and musicians, monkeys and dancing bears.

A dancing bear

A medieval fair

63

Plays

In the Middle Ages people enjoyed watching plays, which, at first, were acted in the church porch. This was how the priests taught the people Bible stories.

Sometimes these religious plays were acted on a cart which went round the town. They were called Miracle Plays.

A Miracle Play, acted on a cart in the streets

Then there were Gild Plays, each acted by members of one gild. The gilds chose stories which suited their trade; the fishmongers, for instance, would act *Jonah and the Whale*.

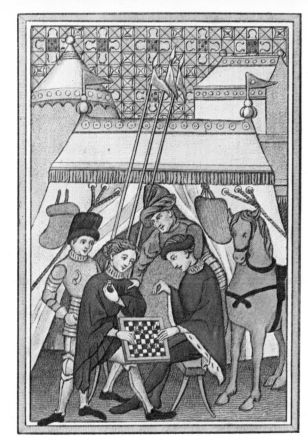

Chess, bowls and cards were favourite pastimes

Games

Children and grown-ups played games, some of which were rather rough. In *hot cockles* one player knelt down blindfold and the others gave him hard whacks until he guessed who it was. *Hoodman blind* was like our blindman's buff, except that one must hit the blind man with a knotted capuchon (hood).

Boys also played *hoop and hide, hide and seek, fillip the toad, ninepins, stoolball* and *barley-break*.

Grown-ups played these games and also football, which was later stopped because so many people were hurt or killed. They liked dancing, and we know they played chess and draughts. The sons of nobles played with jointed soldiers, and girls had dolls.

Fishing

6 Homes in the Later Middle Ages

Manor houses

The first manor-houses, in Norman times, were built with the hall upstairs for safety and an outside staircase. They were draughty and uncomfortable. The only other room, besides the hall, was the lord's solar, or bedroom.

In later days the hall was downstairs and the manor-houses were made more comfortable. There were now several bedrooms, and these were reached by staircases inside the house. Wooden screens kept off draughts from the door.

Large manor-houses had a gallery in the great hall for musicians, who would play to the lord and his noble guests. The king and his court were always travelling about the country, staying first with one lord and then with another.

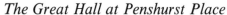

A gittern, the oldest surviving English musical instrument

The Great Hall at Penshurst Place

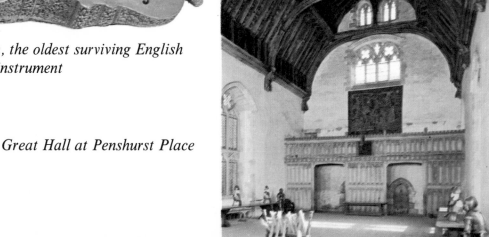

66

The inside walls, instead of being bare stone, were now covered with wooden panels, painted in gay colours, or with tapestries like the one in the picture, which covered much of the walls from floor to ceiling. Many of these were woven in Flanders. The best came from a town called Arras.

A tapestry, woven at Tournai

The floors had tiles and rush mats, in place of dirty rushes, but only the richest people had carpets and these were hung on the walls or spread on tables.

Glass was now being put into the window spaces in nobles' houses. The glass was very costly and was fitted into frames, which were taken down when the lord went away.

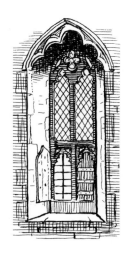

Inside a nobleman's house

The noble family now had a smaller room near the hall called the winter parlour. This was cosier in the winter and was used when there were no important visitors. There was a big fireplace, with a fire of logs on the wide hearth, but there was still very little furniture, even in the richest homes.

The manor-houses in the country still needed a thick wall around them and a moat, and all men, except monks and clerks, had to be ready to fight an unfriendly baron.

The kitchen was now joined to the house by a covered way, and so were the pantry (bread store) and buttery (ale and wine store).

A walled town garden

We first hear of flower gardens about this time, which means that life was a little more peaceful. You can see on this page one of the earliest pictures of a town garden.

Merchants' houses

In the towns, merchants lived above their shops and workrooms. They had a fine panelled living-room with a large fireplace, and if they were rich, glass filled the window spaces. On the floor they had rush mats. Their servants hung fresh green branches on the walls for decoration.

The apprentices, who always lived in their masters' house, slept in the shop, often curled up under the counter.

Geoffrey Kidwelly, a merchant.
Notice his purse and prayer beads

Inside a merchant's house

A bedroom

This merchant and his guest are in the living-room. They have finished dinner and are now discussing business. Notice the wide bench on which they are sitting, with its cushioned seat and high wooden back.

The merchant's solar, or bedroom, was over the living-room. It jutted out over the street. (The servants could easily throw water down into the street gutter from here.)

The bed was the most important piece of furniture, with its feather mattress, and its curtains to pull all round at night.

There was also a cradle for the baby and, under the big bed, a truckle bed on wheels to be pulled out at night for a lady's maid-servant.

A strong box, or coffer, was often kept at the foot of the bed, in which were stored money, jewels and important papers, for there were no banks where a man might keep his valuables safely.

70

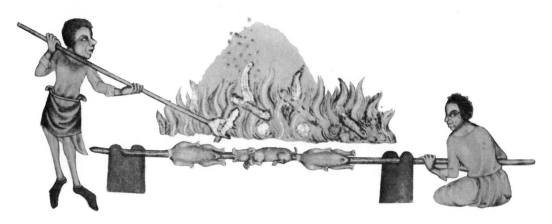

Food and cooking

Cooking on a spit

Every manor-house had a large kitchen with
several fireplaces. There were many cooks and
scullion boys, each with their own special job.
They had to prepare meals for all the people who
lived in a manor-house—perhaps fifty persons,
and visitors also.

A water-jug

Joints of fresh meat, perhaps venison, chickens and geese, were roasted in front of the fire on a spit, which was turned by a scullion boy. When the birds were done, they were served at table, from the spit.

Salted meat, which was eaten in winter, was boiled in large cauldrons, and served as stew.

At this time, ovens came into use. An oven was a big space in the thick wall, with an iron door. A bundle of faggots was put inside and lighted. When all the sticks had burned out, the door was opened and the ashes were raked to one side. Bread, pies and cakes were put inside. The door was shut and by the time the oven was cool, they were cooked.

Ovens came into use in kitchens at this time

In smaller houses and in peasants' cottages, they made an oven by pushing aside the ashes of a hot wood fire, and putting the pie down on the hearth under an iron cover. Hot ashes were then piled on top.

Meat, cheese and bread were the chief foods. (There were still no potatoes.) Herrings, eels and salted fish were very common in winter. Spices, such as ginger, cinnamon and saffron, were used by the rich to make their food more tasty.

Cooking in a cauldron

Cider, beer and wine were drunk, and even the children had beer for breakfast. Fruit was now more popular and apples, pears, peaches and plums were grown. Grape vines often covered the sunny monastery walls, and dates, figs and oranges could be bought at the fair.

The lord of the manor at table

People were very big eaters, as you can see from this menu:

First course: lamprey, codling, mutton, chicken, goose, dove, worts (vegetables) and pastry.

Second course: eels, sea horses, lamb, duck, quail, goldfinches and pie.

On the tables there were now cloths, spoons and knives, a silver salt-cellar and silver or pewter dishes and jugs. Even so, round thick slices of bread called *trenchers* were sometimes used for plates.

Dinner was at 10 or 11 o'clock in the morning and lasted a long time.

Medieval jugs

73

Ploughing

Poor people's homes

The peasants' homes, or cotts, were made of wattle and daub, with oak beams and thatched roofs. There were two rooms, the bower or bedroom, and a larger living-room, which often had a stable at one end. The fire-place, with a stone slab or iron fireback, was now against the wall.

It had a rough chimney-hood to lead the smoke out. The peasants had very little furniture. Their food was still bread, vegetables, eggs and sometimes a little meat. They began work when it was light, and went on until sunset, except on holy days, when everyone enjoyed themselves.

Clearing land for farming

Children

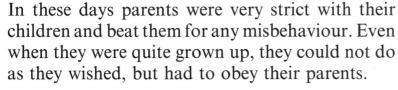

A page serving at table

An engaged couple

In these days parents were very strict with their children and beat them for any misbehaviour. Even when they were quite grown up, they could not do as they wished, but had to obey their parents.

The sons of nobles were sent to another lord when they were seven years old. They lived in his manor or castle as pages, learning good manners and how to wait at table.

Using a spinning wheel

The girls learned how to manage a big house and how to make medicines from herbs, called simples. They also did beautiful needlework and spinning, and in time the unmarried ones were called spinsters.

Parents arranged marriages without asking their children. Girls were often married at fourteen or sixteen, and it was quite a disgrace to be unmarried at twenty.

A school

Looking after the sheep

There were a few schools (such as Eton and Winchester), but rich men's children were more often taught at home by a tutor, who was a monk or family priest. He took prayers at home and usually wrote all the letters.

Peasants' children did not go to school, but a few were sent to the monastery as novices, to be trained as monks.

Sometimes priests taught the children Bible stories in the church porch.

By the time peasants' children were seven years old, most of them were minding the animals and helping their fathers. Only rarely was a poor boy allowed to go to the monastery school to learn to read and write. If he was lucky, he might become a clerk or bailiff on the manor.

Yet More Happenings 7

Henry IV, who had taken away the crown from Richard II, tried to rule the country well and the barons were more peaceable.

His son, Henry V, was a famous soldier-king. He restarted the war with France, which had gone on for so long that it was known as the Hundred Years' War.

Henry took a small army across the Channel and attacked the French. He won a remarkable victory at Agincourt in 1415, when the English archers proved their skill against the heavily armed French knights.

Henry V

A sea battle in the Hundred Years War

*English archers at
Agincourt*

Joan of Arc

The archers stood behind a row of pointed stakes. The French knights on horseback charged, but they could not pass the stakes and their horses stumbled and fell. The archers fired arrows from their long-bows, and the arrows fell like rain among the French.

After this victory, Henry ruled most of France, but he died at an early age.

Henry V was followed by his young son, who, as Henry VI, grew up to be a good man, but a feeble king. The French, led by Joan of Arc, soon won back their country, except the town of Calais.

When Henry VI fell ill, the barons began to quarrel. There were two parties, the House of York and the House of Lancaster, each trying to seize the king's power. As a sign of their party, men wore roses—white for York and red for Lancaster, so these wars between the barons and their followers are called the Wars of the Roses.

The Earl of Warwick, known as Warwick the Kingmaker, was a very powerful baron. Although he won a great victory and made Edward IV king, the wars still went on.

Another important man of this time was William Caxton. When he was a merchant in Flanders, he learned of a new invention—the printing press. In 1476 he set up a printing press of his own in Westminster. This press could print many copies of a book. One of the first books to be printed was Chaucer's *Canterbury Tales*.

Until this time all books were written by hand, by the monks and clerks, so each one took a very long time. A printing press could produce books much more quickly.

Twelve year-old Edward V was murdered in the Tower of London, probably by order of his uncle, who became Richard III.

The long Wars of the Roses ended when Richard was killed in battle, in 1485 and Henry Tudor became king. He was Henry VII, first of the great Tudors. This is the end of the time known as the Middle Ages.

A printing press

An example of Caxton's printing

A king and his army enter a town

79

Index

Looking at History   R J Unstead

Book Three

Tudors and Stuarts

Adam and Charles Black   London

Acknowledgements

Trustees of the British Museum   8b, 41b, 43a, b & c, 80a
Curator of the City Museum & Art Gallery, Plymouth   18a, 19a
Department of the Environment   6a, 10a, 15a, 57b
Derbyshire Countryside Ltd   59b, 95
Edinburgh University Library   41a, 67b, 70a
Mary Evans Picture Library   16c, 33a, 35a, b & c, 37a, b & c, 45a, 64, 67a, 73a, 82b
Guildhall Museum   17c
Trustees of the London Museum   36c, 46a & b, 50a, b, d & e, 51a, b, d & e, 52b,
   c & d, 54d, 60a & b, 62b, 74a & b
Magdalene College, Cambridge   25
Mansell Collection   3, 4a & b, 5b, 6b, c & d, 7c, 10b, 13a, b & c, 15b, 16a & b, 18b,
   20b, 21a, 22b, 23, 24, 26b, 28b, 30a, 32a, 33c & d, 34a, 37d, 38b, 39a, 40b,
   44a, b & c, 47b, 48b, 49c, 50c, 52a, 54b, 56c & d, 62a, 63a & b, 65b, c & d, 69a,
   76, 78b, 80b, 82a, 83b, 86, 87c, 88b, 89a & b, 91a & b, 92, 93a, b, c, d, e, f & g, 94b
Marquess of Salisbury & Photo Precision Ltd   10c, 11a
National Buildings Record   54a
National Gallery, London   90
National Maritime Museum, London   27, 72b
National Portrait Gallery   5d
National Trust   12a, 58b
Crown Copyright, Public Record Office   5c, 49a
Radio Times Hulton Picture Library   20a
Henry Trivick (from his book *Brasses in Gilt* published by John Baker)   2
Victoria & Albert Museum   5a, 8a, 14a & b, 17a, 32b, 56b, 58a, 59a
P F White   9a, 11b, 12b, 18c
Woodmansterne Ltd & National Maritime Museum, London   7a & b, 22a, 26a, 28a,
   47a, 55, 56a, 57a & c, 71a & b, 72a, 94a, cover
Photographs 1 & 31a are reproduced by permission of Viscount De l'Isle, VC KG,
   Penshurst Place, Kent
Photographs 48a & 88a are reproduced by gracious permission of Her Majesty the
   Queen
The drawings in this book are by J C B Knight, Doreen Roberts and others
Designed by Karen Bowen

Published by A & C Black (Publishers) Ltd
35 Bedford Row London WC1R 4JH

ISBN 0 7136 1422 6 limp
     0 7136 1418 8 net
     0 7136 1572 9 complete edition of Books 1–5

First published in this edition 1974. Reprinted 1975, 1977, 1978 & 1979
©1974 A & C Black Ltd
Previous editions © 1953, 1961 A & C Black Ltd

Printed in Great Britain by Sir Joseph Causton & Sons Ltd
London and Eastleigh

Contents

The Tudor Kings and Queens 1

Henry VII came to the throne in 1485, and the people, who had grown tired of so much fighting and unrest during the Wars of the Roses, were glad to have a king who would keep peace in the country. Henry forced the barons to obey the law, and he helped merchants to trade more peacefully. He was fond of wealth, and by introducing new taxes and fines he amassed large sums of money for the Crown.

Henry VII

When Henry VII died, in 1509, his son Henry VIII became king. He was a masterful king, clever and rich and he liked to have his own way in all things.

Until this time, everyone in England was a Catholic. The Pope, who lived in Rome, was the head of the Catholic Church, and the kings and princes were subject to him. Henry VIII wished to divorce his wife, Katharine of Aragon, so that he could marry Anne Boleyn. The Pope would not allow him to do so, and they quarrelled. Henry disobeyed the Pope and married Anne.

Anne Boleyn

Gold seal of Henry VIII

Henry VIII

Armour made for Henry VIII

He ordered the monasteries to be pulled down, and seized their lands and riches. Then he made himself head of the Church of England. This behaviour horrified the Catholics, who were still loyal to the Pope in Rome, but they were unable to overthrow so strong a king.

Henry VIII was married six times, and of his children only three survived him: Edward, Mary and Elizabeth. Edward was a delicate boy of nine when he became King Edward VI. He died six years later, and his elder sister, Mary, became queen. Mary was a faithful Catholic and during her reign she did everything in her power to make England a Roman Catholic country.

There were many people who would not accept the Pope's authority: they were called Protestants. In Mary's reign nearly three hundred were put to death. Among them were Archbishop Cranmer, and Bishops Hooper, Ridley and Latimer, who were burnt at the stake. It has to be remembered that, in these times, both Protestants and Catholics suffered for their religious beliefs.

Mary died after only five years as queen, and was followed by the greatest of the Tudors, Queen Elizabeth I, who reigned from 1558-1603.

Edward VI

Queen Mary

Protestants burnt at the stake

Elizabeth was a clever woman whose chief aims in life were to keep her throne and to make England a strong country. The Queen made England Protestant again. She was not popular with the Catholics and there were several plots against her life.

Queen Elizabeth

For the first thirty years of Elizabeth's reign, England was at peace, although it was not easy to keep on friendly terms with Spain. King Philip of Spain was angry with England, for at least three reasons:

1 Because England refused to obey the Pope. As a good Catholic he thought it was his duty to try and alter this.
2 Because Elizabeth secretly sent help to the Dutch to enable them to rebel against their Spanish rulers.
3 Because Francis Drake, Richard Grenville and other sea-dogs robbed his treasure ships on their way home from the New World (America). Philip and the Pope had decided that the New World belonged only to Spain. In 1588, after many years of uneasy peace, Philip sent a mighty Armada of 130 ships to invade England.

The English had smaller vessels but their guns were heavier. These guns crippled many of the Spanish ships, others were destroyed by fireships or gales and less than half of the Spanish fleet returned to port.

Philip II of Spain

*A plate, in honour
of Queen Elizabeth*

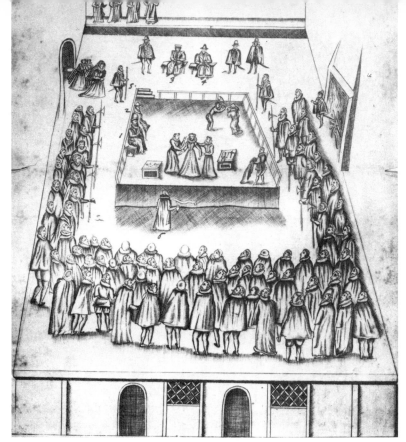

The execution of Mary, Queen of Scots

Shakespeare

Spenser

Mary, Queen of Scots, Elizabeth's cousin, was a most unfortunate woman. The Scots turned her off the throne and she fled to England where Elizabeth kept her prisoner for nineteen years. She became the centre of Catholic plots and Elizabeth finally agreed to her execution.

Elizabeth's reign was a glorious period in English history. It produced men of great daring and enterprise: Sir Francis Drake, Sir Richard Grenville and John Hawkins, and men who wrote poetry, plays and books that are still read today.

The greatest of these writers was William Shakespeare, the playwright. Other playwrights were Christopher Marlowe and Ben Jonson. The poets included Philip Sidney and Edmund Spenser, and among the other famous men of letters were Francis Bacon, Walter Raleigh and Richard Hakluyt, who described the *Principal Voyages* of his time. Elizabeth was a great queen who understood her people, both rich and poor. Let us see how they lived in Tudor times.

Tudor Homes 2

Framework of a Tudor house

How they built their houses

In Tudor times, as the country became more prosperous, many new houses, both great and small, were built. It was the fashion for the nobles to build large country houses. Most Tudor houses were built on a wooden framework, which was usually made of oak. When the framework was built, the floor-boards of each storey jutted out a little, so that the houses leaned towards each other, across the street.

Here you can see how the 'top sawyer' and the 'bottom sawyer' cut the trunk into planks. Carpenters made the planks and posts smooth with an adze. The spaces in the oak frame were filled in with wattle and plaster, or with red bricks made of clay. These dark red bricks were the newest building material.

Sawyers

Using an adze

Tudor cottages. The chimneys are probably not the original ones

Chimneys at Hampton Court, and one of the gateways

The ends of the roof and the gables were decorated with carved boards. The roof itself was covered with thatch, or tiles. Chimneys were now very tall and were built in attractive shapes.

Palaces, colleges and the biggest manor-houses were usually built entirely of brick or stone. Cardinal Wolsey's great house, Hampton Court, was built of the new red brick. Like Knole and Hatfield House, it is one of the great English houses of this period.

Hatfield House, built just after Queen Elizabeth's death

Inside Tudor houses

At first, the hall was still the chief room. It was usually two storeys high, with a fine staircase leading to the gallery. This gallery was used by musicians, and sometimes by the ladies to watch the gentlemen at dinner.

There were handsome stone fireplaces, with decorated firebacks. In each fireplace a log fire burned in an iron basket. Rich people had glass windows, but glass was still so rare and expensive that the whole window-frame was taken out when the owner moved to another house.

The walls were covered with wooden panelling which was sometimes painted, though fine tapestry was still popular. Door posts, sideboards, and especially the new staircases, were wonderfully carved. Even the ceilings were decorated with plaster patterns and pictures.

The hall of an Elizabethan mansion

Queen Hoo Hall in Hertfordshire, an Elizabethan manor house

Notice the magnificent carving of this staircase, and the gates which kept hunting dogs from going upstairs

11

A long gallery at Knole

Compton Wynyates in Warwickshire

Brick building at Compton Wynyates

Carpets from the East were so valuable that they were hung on the walls or put over tables, rather than on the floor. Floors were made of stone slabs, or were tiled. They were covered with rushes, lavender or rush mats.

It was the custom to hang leafy branches or bunches of lavender on the walls, to make the air smell sweeter. Because of the lack of drainage and piped water, there were many unpleasant smells.

In Elizabeth's reign, oak began to get scarce, because so many new houses were built. Wood was also used for many other things such as ships, furniture, tools and waggons. Most fires burnt wood only; coal was rarely used in houses.

Many of the big new houses were built in the shape of a capital E (perhaps in honour of Elizabeth). The short middle stroke was the entrance porch. The great hall became less important, but it was still a magnificent way into the house. People now preferred smaller rooms: a parlour and a dining-room, bedrooms upstairs and kitchens at the back of the house. The finest room was upstairs. It ran the whole length of the house and so was called the long gallery. The ladies walked in the long gallery when it was too muddy for them to go out in their long, rich dresses. Here, too, the children played and were given lessons by the family priest.

Tudor Homes

The Tudors were very fond of music and singing, and the whole family and guests often gathered in the long gallery to sing and play on musical instruments such as the lute, viol, flute and virginals or spinet, an early type of piano. Other instruments which they played were the recorder, shawm and organ.

Henry VIII was himself an accomplished musician and composer. Many Elizabethan songs, called madrigals, are still popular today.

Playing the virginals

Music was very important to the Tudors, in church (left) and in the home (below)

*A sideboard and
a table*

*Below: an oak chair,
and a walnut bed*

Furniture

In these days furniture became more comfortable and was better made. Tables were no longer just plain trestle-tables, but they had richly carved legs. Most houses now had a few chairs, some, perhaps, with arms.

Chests, sideboards and stools were decorated with carvings and were so well made that a few still exist. Although there was more furniture, rooms in these big houses were very bare compared with those of today. For instance, a house belonging to Sir Henry Parker had only:

2 chairs in the whole house	7 cupboards
8 stools and forms	3 carpets
2 square tables	13 candlesticks
a pair of 'playing tables'	fireshovels and tongs
12 bedsteads, tapestry and bedhangings, feather beds, bolsters, blankets and cushions of velvet and satin	a basin and jug of pewter 6 glasses 6 plates for fruit 2 pewter plates for tarts 1 stool of black velvet, 'for my lady'
3 great chests	

As houses had no corridors upstairs, and people went through one room to get to another, the four-poster beds had curtains to pull round at night.

A Tudor-style garden at Hampton Court

A knot, or design for a garden with many flower beds separated by tiny hedges of clipped box

Gardens

People now began to plan and cultivate gardens, which shows that times were more peaceful. Tudor gardens were very trim, with straight paths, and clipped yew hedges. Flower-beds were of many fancy shapes, and were filled with sweet herbs such as rosemary and lavender. Apricots, oranges, currants and grapes were also grown. There is still a Tudor garden at Hampton Court, which is shown in the photograph above.

The Tudors loved a joke and they sometimes planted a maze in which guests could lose their way for hours. Fountains were hidden in the gardens and squirted water over people as they passed by.

A gardener at work in a herb garden

Two 16th century kitchens. The one above is in a large household, and the one on the left is for a smaller family

Cooking and eating

The Tudors ate large meals of rich food, and dinner, made up of many courses, often lasted for three hours!

Breakfast was only a snack—a mug of beer and a piece of bread, as it was followed by dinner at 11 o'clock in the morning. 'Rere supper', in the evening, became a banquet in the big houses, for Henry VIII loved feasting and merry-making, with fancy costumes, masks, mummers, music and games.

Everyone, except the very poorest folk, ate a great deal of meat and thought vegetables rather poor stuff. Meat was roasted on long spits, turned by the scullion boys, or it was put in an iron box and placed in the hot ashes.

Barrels of meat and fish still had to be salted down for the winter, and a housewife kept enough food in her storeroom for a household of perhaps fifty persons, and for large parties of visitors who might stay for a week or two.

Preparing a hare for cooking

Spices, such as pepper, cloves, ginger and mace, were used to flavour the tough salt meat which had to be eaten in winter. Figs, raisins, almonds and dates came from abroad.

Cakes, jellies, custards and sweets of every kind and shape were popular. Elizabeth's teeth are said to have gone black from eating too many sweets! The name for sweets was comfits; there were 'kissing comfits' for making the breath smell sweeter! Honey was much used and was often poured over meat.

The chief drinks were ale, cider, perry and wine. Tea and coffee were almost unknown. Wines, warmed, sweet and spiced, were favourite drinks. A wine called sack was drunk from a cup half-filled with sugar.

Sir Walter Raleigh brought potatoes from America, but they were not yet widely grown in England. Potato-pie was a special treat. Sugar, made from sugar-cane and sold in big hard 'loaves', took the place of honey in well-to-do homes.

As England became richer, in Elizabeth's reign, plates of silver and pewter took the place of wooden platters and trenchers. There were no china plates yet, but crockery called Delft Ware came from Holland.

An Elizabethan glass cup

While the rich drank from silver and pewter cups, or glasses from Venice, the ordinary folk still poured their beer from a leather jug into mugs of horn. A guest was expected to bring his own knife to dinner, and sometimes a spoon as well, but no-one used forks until late in Elizabeth's reign.

An Elizabethan family at table

The mattress was laid across ropes, rather than springs

Many Tudor houses survive. The timbers used not to be painted, and were often plastered over, as on the right below

The homes of merchants and farmers

The merchants in the towns and the farmers and yeomen in the country built themselves better homes, but the older folk grumbled about the new chimneys, because they thought that smoky rooms were more healthy!

Since large panes of glass were very rare, windows were made up of small diamond-shaped panes set in lead.

Until this time most people slept on straw mattresses and often used a log of wood for a bolster. Now they began to have more comfortable beds, with feather mattresses and pillows, and woollen blankets. The mattress was laid, not on springs, but across ropes. The bed itself was handsomely carved, with, perhaps, the family crest on the headboard.

Even ordinary citizens began to have more furniture in their homes. There might be an armchair for the head of the house, a wooden settle by the fire and a dresser for his wife's new plates. The children and servants sat on stools.

Peasants' homes

The peasants' huts usually had only one or two rooms, with a loft above, made by laying boards across the rafters. The floor was of earth hardened with bull's blood, and the fire, on its hearthstone, had a hood made of basket-work smeared with clay to take the smoke out of the smoke-hole.

It is well to remember that during all the glories of Queen Elizabeth's reign, most English people still lived in the country, working on their own land or on the lord's estate, and seldom leaving their tiny villages.

Notice the warming pan which was filled with hot coals and put into the bed to warm it

The only furniture in a hut like this was a couple of stools, a few pots and a wooden chest

19

3 Sailors and Ships in Tudor Days

A warship of the 15th century

John Cabot

A 16th century ship

Sailors

Christopher Columbus, in his ship, the *Santa Maria*, discovered America in 1492 for the King of Spain. This gave Spain a great Empire and made her the richest country in Europe.

After a time, English sailors began to sail across the Atlantic to the New World, where they were constantly fighting the Spaniards, who claimed that no-one else had a right to be there. Sometimes the English went to trade, but usually they went to rob the Spanish treasure ships bringing home silver from Peru and Mexico, or to attack the Spanish forts and towns on the islands and mainland.

John Cabot, only five years after Columbus's famous voyage, was sent by Henry VII to try to find a way to Cathay (China) and India. He discovered Newfoundland and Labrador, with their rich fishing-grounds, but he did not find the silver and gold for which he had hoped. This disappointment caused the English to lose interest in the New World for a few years.

Vol. VI. Pl. XXII. p. 208.

Tunnage... 1000.

MEN
Soldiers 349
Mariners .... 301 } 700
Gunners 50

Henry VIII took an interest in ships, and founded the Royal Navy. His ship, *The Great Harry*, was the finest ship of the time, and it was fitted with cannons which were fired through port-holes.

William Hawkins sailed under King Henry's flag to Guinea in West Africa. Sir John Hawkins, his son, started the Slave Trade in Elizabeth's reign. He sailed to West Africa where he bought or captured black people. He took them by ship across the Atlantic, and sold them to the Spaniards for work on the sugar plantations and in the silver mines. In those days, nobody thought this was cruel.

The 'Great Harry'. The crew was 301 sailors, 50 gunners and 349 soldiers

Henry VIII's fleet at Dover in 1520

During Elizabeth's reign, the greatest English seaman was Francis Drake. After several previous voyages, he set out in 1577 from Plymouth with five ships: the *Pelican, Elizabeth, Swan, Marygold* and *Benedict*, which were small vessels, but wonderfully fitted out with fine guns, rich furniture and silver plate. They crossed the Atlantic and sailed south. Four of the ships either turned back or were lost, but Drake sailed on alone in the 120-ton *Pelican*, which he renamed the *Golden Hind*.

Despite a mutiny and storms, Drake entered the Pacific and fell upon the unwary Spaniards, robbing their ships and filling his own with treasure. From San Francisco (or New Albion) he sailed ever westward to the Spice Islands, the East Indies and Africa, reaching England at last, after three years, with treasure worth a million pounds.

This was the most glorious voyage an Englishman had ever made, and it stirred the hearts of English sailors. (Magellan's ship, the *Victoria*, had sailed round the world fifty-five years earlier, but Ferdinand Magellan, the Portuguese captain, was killed on the voyage.)

Sir Francis Drake

Map of Drake's voyage round the world

22

Other famous Elizabethan sailors

Martin Frobisher was sent by the Queen to find the way to Cathay, by sailing north around America. He searched bravely in the icy seas for this North-west Passage, but in vain. He made three voyages and brought back cargoes of black stones supposed to contain gold, but they were valueless. John Davis made further explorations, but he, also, could not find the Passage.

Henry Hudson, in James I's reign, explored farther still, but his disappointed crew mutinied and set him adrift in a little boat. He was never heard of again. Men dreamed for years of this North-west Passage, this quick way to China. (There *is* a. way through, but the ice makes it useless for trading ships.)

Sir Walter Raleigh and Sir Humphrey Gilbert had the idea of making colonies for English people, where they could settle down and make homes in the New World. Gilbert started a colony in Newfoundland but it failed, and he decided to return home. He did not reach England, as his little ship *Squirrel* was wrecked on the way.

Sir John Hawkins traded in slaves

Sir Walter Raleigh, who made unsuccessful attempts to start colonies in Virginia and elsewhere. He fought the Spaniards and searched constantly for El Dorado—the land of gold. Raleigh was executed by James I for his part in a plot

23

Sir Richard Grenville, as fierce and courageous as a lion, sailed against the Spaniards countless times. He died of wounds after his ship, the *Revenge* had fought a Spanish fleet of fifty-three ships all day and all night.

Besides these famous seamen, there were many other adventurers:

Sebastian Cabot, son of John Cabot, was a map-maker who claimed that he explored the American coast as far as Florida. Later he started the Merchant Adventurers' Company, which sent Sir Hugh Willoughby to find the North-east Passage (that is, a way round Lapland and Russia) to India. The expedition failed to find a way and Willoughby perished, but his chief officer, Richard Chancellor, reached Moscow and traded with the Russians. The Muscovy Company continued this trade for many years.

Russian and English merchants

Another company of merchants, called the Levant Company, braved the Mediterranean pirates to trade with Venice and Turkey. One of them, Ralph Fitch, travelled overland to China. After eight years he came home, to tell of strange new lands and of great chances of trade in spices, cloth and rare Eastern goods. To encourage this trade, Elizabeth granted a charter to the East India Company.

The adventurous spirit of the men mentioned in these pages successfully increased English trade in all parts of the world. Ships left port heavily laden with cloth, hardware and firearms, and in return brought back produce from abroad —new foods, new materials and precious stones. English merchants became rich and important.

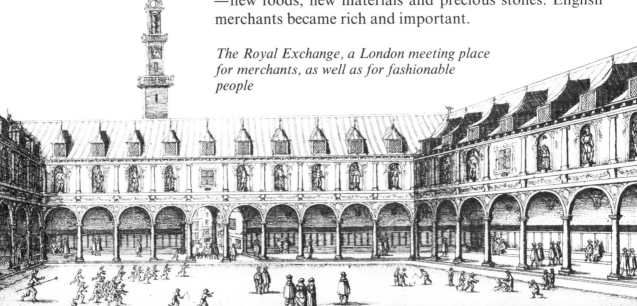

The Royal Exchange, a London meeting place for merchants, as well as for fashionable people

Shipwrights working on a design

Ships

A Viking ship had a beaked prow and one square sail. It was steered by a big oar, as you can see in the picture on the right. At the time of the Crusades a deck was added and little 'castles' at the stern (back) and bow (foreward). Steering was still by means of an oar.

When the Portuguese and Spaniards began their discoveries, and later, when the English began to explore the world, larger and stronger ships were built, which would stand up to ocean voyages.

Look at the picture of the *Golden Hind*. It has three masts, called fore (front), main (middle) and mizzen (stern) masts. The big square sail in the middle is called the mainsail, and there is a little one above called a topsail. The foremast had its foresail and also a small topsail, which is furled (rolled up). The mizzen mast has a triangular sloping sail called a lateen.

Look again at the *Golden Hind*. She has a beaked prow and above it, the forecastle (though it is no longer very much like a castle). This was where the sailors slept. Then come three decks, the lowest called the main-deck.

Rising up towards the stern is the quarter-deck, and above this at the stern the poop-deck, where the captain had his rooms. In this way the stern of ships in Tudor times became rather like a three-storeyed house.

A Viking longship and the 'Golden Hind'

A ship of Stuart times, the 'Resolution', in a gale

By the time of the Armada, the Spanish ships had fore-castles, and poops which towered out of the sea, but the English ships were now less clumsy and were lower in the water.

The 'Ark Royal', flagship of the English fleet which defeated the Armada

The *Ark Royal*, shown below, was the flagship of the English fleet which defeated the Spanish Armada. She was a ship of 800 tons—large for that time. The third sails above the topsails are called top-gallants. Notice the port-holes for the cannons, and the lantern on the stern. The mast at the prow or beak is the bowsprit.

The 'Sovereign of the Seas'. Notice how much gilding there is on the stern

The ships of Stuart times still had high poops, but the middle of the ship now had an upper deck above the main deck, so that the 'waist' in the middle could not be seen.

Ships like the *Royal Prince* (1610) and the *Sovereign of the Seas* had a carved figure on the beak. There were also carvings round the stern. Ships were brightly painted and gilded, and the captain and his officers had richly furnished cabins.

27

A ship in Naples harbour. The tall building is a lighthouse

Sailors

A ship, about 1610

Although the officers lived under comfortable conditions, life for the ordinary seaman was very hard, and it continued to be so for hundreds of years. The sailors had their quarters in the forecastle, where there was barely room to lie down. In rough weather everything became soaking wet and there was always the smell of bilge water from the hold below.

The ordinary seamen had very poor food. They lived on bread, cheese, salted meat and salted fish, which soon rotted in the heat and damp below decks. As they had no fresh vegetables when at sea, sailors often suffered from a skin disease called scurvy.

After a few days at sea drinking water became stale and unhealthy, and on long voyages it was strictly rationed. Ships put in to shore for fresh water whenever possible. It is not surprising that only the bravest and hardiest men could survive this kind of life, and they were often rough and brutal too.

Trading ships, or merchantmen, were very similar to warships, as all ships were armed at this time. The English fleet, which fought against the Armada, was chiefly made up of small merchant ships. Cargo was carried in the hold, which was reached from the main deck by openings called hatchways.

How the People Lived in Tudor Times

How they dressed

From these pictures of noble people in Henry VIII's reign, you can see how rich and gay clothes were, compared with those of today. The man with a hawk on his finger is wearing a short velvet cloak, lined with fur. His rich doublet is open in front to show his silk shirt underneath. His sleeves are padded and slit, and there are layers of rich linings.

He is wearing short breeches and velvet stockings with wide, open shoes. There were many different kinds of hat, but this flat one, with a feather, was especially popular.

His lady as you can see, wears a heavy dress of velvet, embroidered in wonderful patterns with silver thread. Notice her big sleeves and damask petticoat. Her necklace and belt are made of gold, and she has jewels sewn on to her hat.

Here are some of the styles in hats. Notice how fond people were of fur trimmings

Ladies of Henry VIII's Court

A Tudor family

Servants

Poorer people wore clothes made of rough woollen cloth, or coarse cotton, called fustian. A peasant or workman had a shirt, loose breeches and leggings bound crosswise with straps. He often had a belted jerkin on top. A better-off farmer wore a leather doublet and hose. Cloaks were worn in cold weather.

Peasant women and servants wore a dress with a fairly short skirt, and an apron. Their stockings were made of cloth and tied above the knee. Caps were made of white wool.

People could not buy ready-made clothes. Housewives and, in big houses, sewing-women made all the clothes by hand. Here is a rich family of the same time. Notice that children were dressed in the same style as grown-ups.

Market women and a water-carrier

Dancing at Court

In Elizabeth's reign the dress at Court was the richest in English history. Ladies and gentlemen now began to wear ruffs round their necks. These were made of white cambric and were sometimes held in place by wires.

Gentlemen wore padded breeches or trunks, which became so enormous that it was difficult to sit down. Their tight-fitting tunics, or doublets, were covered with fine embroidery and were often slashed to show the rich lining beneath. Pointed beards were very fashionable.

Shoes were made of leather and were often tied round the ankles

Men carried swords and daggers

In the picture on the left, just before the time of the Armada, you can see the man's short cloak, made of velvet or scented leather. His doublet was quilted and padded so that his chest stuck out.

The lady's dress has a tight bodice with padded sleeves, rich embroidery and an underskirt of patterned damask or satin. White collars and ruffs were now stiffened with starch, a new idea from Holland.

Ladies' dresses were padded and made to stand out over a frame or hoop, which was fastened round the waist. The great skirt was stretched over a frame of whalebone called a farthingale

Sir Christopher Hatton, a gentleman at Queen Elizabeth's Court

Some Elizabethan hat styles for men

32

A merchant and his family

Ordinary folk were not allowed to dress like the nobles. A wealthy merchant wore a long gown of dark, rich, cloth, but compared with the courtiers he was very plainly dressed. His wife also wore simple clothes and often a Dutch cap, like the one in the picture.

A page

Servants were dressed usually in blue, and wore their master's badge in silver on the arm. Apprentice lads had blue gowns, white breeches and flat woollen caps. They were forbidden by law to wear ruffs, jewels, embroidered shoes, or fancy garters. If they disobeyed, they could be publicly whipped.

A noblewoman, a citizen's wife and a young man, of 1570

A London merchant

A countryman with a pack and a brace of rabbits

A beggar

Footpads made it unsafe to walk in the streets at night

Poor people and beggars

Although England was growing richer there was a large number of poor and hungry people. This was chiefly because:

Rich men had made enclosures, by fencing in the common land for their own use.

Many more sheep were kept, which meant that fewer farm workers were needed to till the soil.

The monasteries, which had cared for the poor, had been closed so there was less help for the hungry.

The population was increasing, but there was not enough food and work for everybody. Every parish had to look after its poor and provide materials so that they could work in the 'workhouse'.

Poor people and 'sturdy rogues' wandered about the country as beggars, or in robber bands, until London and the countryside became unsafe. Elizabeth made laws to help the poor, so that more corn was grown and more cattle kept instead of sheep.

Punishments

As the country was so full of rogues, vagabonds and robbers, it seemed necessary to have many severe punishments. Here are some of the most common.

Murderers were boiled alive or burned to death; robbers had one or both ears cut off and noses slit open; sheep-stealers had their hands cut off; vagabonds were whipped in the stocks or through the streets, and scolds were ducked in the water in a ducking-stool. Rogues were put in the pillory and were often branded with a red-hot iron.

Thieves were known as 'cut-purses', because they cut the leather straps which fastened a purse to the belt. 'Hookers' were thieves who carried long poles to hook goods out of windows, which was not very difficult, as houses were so close together.

A popular man did not find the stocks too much of a punishment

The pillory   *A ducking-stool*

Soldiers

As you can see from the pictures, armour was still worn, consisting of a breastplate, thigh-guards and a helmet, but it was lighter than that used during the Hundred Years' War. The nobles had fine armour, but it gave little protection against bullets.

Pikeman and archers

A helmet of the Elizabethan period

Archers wore a padded tunic, while ordinary soldiers, who did not yet wear a uniform, usually had a leather jerkin. The longbow was still used, because the early guns—muskets, arquebus and matchlocks—were so slow and heavy. Thirty or forty shots an hour was thought to be quite fast shooting. Soldiers carried a forked stick to rest their guns on when firing them.

Archer, musketeer and pikeman

The pikemen, with pikes over 6 metres long, protected the archers and musketeers in battle. Every village and town had to find archers, gunmen, pikemen and billmen in time of war, as well as armour and shirts of mail for the Royal Army.

Guns and cannons were becoming larger and heavier and were used for land sieges and sea battles

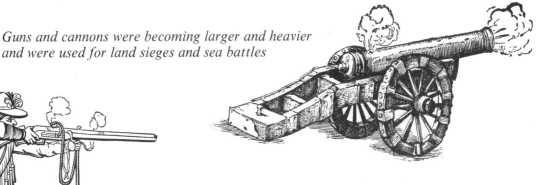

Tobacco was sold in pennyworths. For twopence a man could buy enough to fill his pocket. Cigarettes were not yet thought of

Smoking

Smoking was unknown in England until Elizabeth's reign, when Sir Walter Raleigh returned from one of his long voyages to the New World with a cargo of tobacco. The habit of smoking soon spread and even ladies were to be seen smoking clay pipes!

At the theatre a man lit his pipe and passed it to his lady. In the evenings he often went to the tavern to meet his friends and to smoke. It is said that even the children were taught by their schoolmasters to smoke, and to blow the smoke down their noses!

An inn scene with card-players

At the theatre

During the Middle Ages people became fond of watching plays, which were either acted in the church porch or on a cart. In Elizabethan times they used inn-yards for play-acting, and people watched the performance from the balconies surrounding the yard, while others stood in the yard itself. The actors travelled about from place to place, and as they usually stayed at the inn, the yard of the inn was a most convenient place for them to perform in.

The first theatres were built in the shape of inn-yards, with three rows of balconies round a courtyard. A roof covered the balconies, but the courtyard or 'pit' was open to the sky. The stage, as you can see on page 40, was built out into the pit. It was quite common for some of the young gallants to sit on the stage itself.

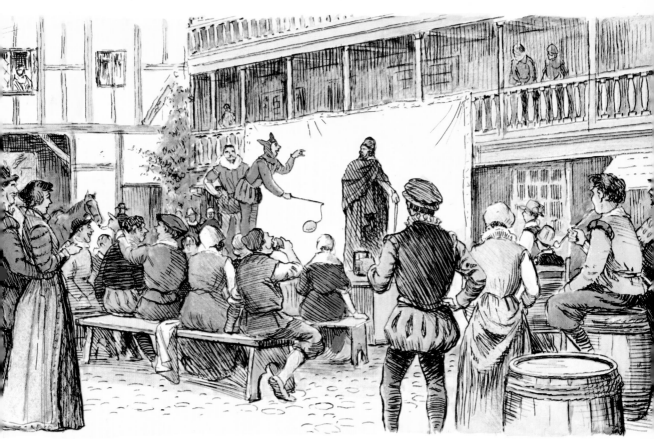

Travelling players performing in an inn-yard

The Fortune at Cripplegate, and *The Swan* and *The Globe* across the Thames at Bankside, Southwark, were some of the earliest theatres. These were built outside the city walls because the Aldermen of London did not favour play-acting.

On a fine afternoon a flag was flown from the top of the theatre, and a trumpeter sounded his trumpet to let everyone know that a play was soon to begin. The audience was always lively, playing dice and cards, and shouting for tobacco, nuts and pots of ale. The poorer folk stood or sat in the pit, and the apprentices especially were very rowdy if they didn't like the play.

On the stage women's parts were taken by boys, and the actors usually wore the ordinary clothes of the time. There was very little scenery.

William Shakespeare, the actor and playwright, lived during the reigns of Elizabeth and James I. Little is known about his life, but it seems that he joined a company of actors called the Lord Chamberlain's Men. He wrote a large number of plays to be performed at *The Globe*.

The Globe, Rose and Bear baiting Theatres, outside the city walls

Bear-baiting

A contemporary picture of the Swan Theatre, Bankside

How the people enjoyed themselves

Another way in which people enjoyed themselves was by going to *The Bear Garden*, a building similar in shape to the theatres. Here they watched mastiff dogs attacking a bull or bear, which was tied to a post. Sometimes men set on a blinded bear with whips.

Cock-fighting was already popular, but it was a cruel sport. We should have preferred to see quarter-staff matches, wrestling or bowls. The London Archers still held their shooting matches out in the fields near the city.

Hunting and hawking were sports for the royal family and the nobles. The picture on the right shows the Queen and her hunting party stopping to picnic in the forest. Notice the boy helping himself to a drink.

A picnic for the Queen when hunting

41

Everyone enjoyed himself on Mayday, Midsummer's Eve, Martinmas, Whitsun and Shrove Tuesday, but Christmas was the merriest, maddest festival of them all.

In big houses there was a Lord of Misrule, who ruled over all the mummers, jesters and merrymakers, and they were forced to obey him in even the wildest pranks. He rode on a hobby-horse and was followed by many attendants wearing heads of strange monsters, or decked in scarves, ribbons and lace, with bells, pipes and drums.

At the Christmas feast, a boar's head was brought in on a great dish, and a peacock pie, decorated with the bird's head and its beautiful outspread tail. There were great joints of meat, geese, mince-pies and plum pudding.

All the servants and poor folk were invited to the feast. Afterwards, when the yule-log had been dragged in, there were merry games, and best of all, dancing.

Preparing for football

Christmas feast at a big house

Queen Elizabeth was fond of dancing, and she practised her dances nearly every day, for there were a great many and some were very difficult. Here are the names of a few of the dances: the Pavane (slow and solemn), the Jig, the Lavolta (a leaping, twisting dance), the Brawl (from France), the lively Galliard, the Fancy and the Ney, which the maids danced in the streets on feast-days.

Cards and dice were favourite indoor winter games. At Court, Elizabeth's courtiers delighted in poetry, singing and music.

How they travelled

Although more people travelled about the country than in the Middle Ages, the roads were still very bad. Farmers took stones up from the road, or dug up the soil and even ploughed across the highway.

The ruts were so deep on main roads that carts might turn over, and in winter, people were even drowned in the deep holes. Travellers had to hire guides to find the way, for there were no signposts or milestones.

Robber bands hid in the woods and attacked travellers in lonely places, so no man dared to travel at night or alone. All men carried weapons, and their friends prayed for them while they were away on a journey.

Robber bands attacked travellers

A village, about 1600. Notice how muddy the road is

No-one troubled to mend the roads unless a Royal Progress (or procession) was coming.

Kings and queens spent much of their time travelling about the country and staying with nobles. When it was known that they were coming on a visit, the townsfolk hurried to mend their part of the highroad and to find horses to pull royal carts. Queen Elizabeth had 400 waggons when she went on her journeys.

Arriving at an inn

When people died they sometimes left money to build a bridge or to have a stone roadway repaired. In former days, monks had built chapels and collected alms to provide guides for lost travellers.

Stage-waggons came into use in Tudor times. They were heavy, lumbering carts, pulled by six, eight or ten horses, and they carried poor folk and goods. The driver walked beside his horses.

Coaches were in use on the Continent for some years before being introduced into England. The first coach is said to have been presented to Queen Elizabeth by a Dutchman about 1565, though it seems possible that Mary possessed an earlier model.

Nonsuch Palace

These early coaches had no springs and were most uncomfortable, so Elizabeth preferred to ride on horseback and only rode in her coach when she came to a town.

Queen Elizabeth arriving at Nonsuch on a progress

A main road, leading to a town. Notice the let-down flap to the window of the coach

The whirlicote with its hinged shutter seems to have been the earliest hackney coach and could be hired in London towards the end of Elizabeth's reign. Travellers could hire horses at inns, ride on about fifteen kilometres to the next inn, leave the horses and hire fresh ones.

Messengers were the only really swift travellers in these days, and the law said that innkeepers must help them, and other travellers must allow them to pass. Great persons had their own messengers to carry letters and news. The Royal Messenger was the most important of all. It took him more than a week to ride from London to Scotland.

Inns were now more comfortable than the ale-houses of earlier days. Rich guests could have table-cloths and clean sheets, and listen to music while eating their meals. An odd custom was for visitors to be kissed by the landlady and her maids when they arrived.

Inside an inn

45

A model of London Bridge. The building which sticks out is a chapel

A model of Cheapside

Tudor London

In Tudor times, London was still a small walled city surrounded by green fields. But as more and more people came to London, and its trade increased, the city became very overcrowded. People then began to build houses outside the city walls and along the river bank towards the palace at Whitehall. To the east, the shacks and hovels outside the walls lay beyond the Lord Mayor's control, and Bankside, south of the river, was famous for its slums and low taverns.

James I

The Stuarts 5

When Elizabeth died in 1603 her cousin, King James VI of Scotland (son of Mary, Queen of Scots), came from Scotland to be King James I. Thus, after centuries of strife and trouble between the two countries, England and Scotland were on the way to becoming united.

In those days men felt that religion was the most important thing in their lives, and they fought and died for it. Under Elizabeth, England had been a Protestant country, but the Catholics hoped that James would favour them.

James did not wish to change the religion of his new country, and a number of Catholics plotted to blow up the Houses of Parliament on a day when he was to be present. The Gunpowder Plot was discovered, and Guy Fawkes, one of the leaders, was executed.

The arrest of Guy Fawkes

The 'Gunpowder Plotters'

Christopher Wright · John Wright · Thomas Percy · Guido Fawkes · Robert Catesby · Thomas Winter

Charles I and his army

A Puritan woman

The Puritans were people who believed in simple worship and plain living. They had no bishops, priests or prayer book, and met together in the plainest of buildings. When they were not allowed to worship as they wished, a number of families, known afterwards as the Pilgrim Fathers, sailed in the *Mayflower* to America.

They started the colony of New England, and in spite of hardships and attacks by Red Indians, they built their homes and made farms.

Charles I became king in 1625. He believed that he should rule England by Divine Right: that is, since God had made him a King, he could rule without the advice of a Parliament. This led to a quarrel between King and Parliament, and Civil War broke out between them.

The King's followers were the Cavaliers, and Parliament's soldiers, many of whom were Puritans, were known as Roundheads, because of their closely cropped hair.

A battle in the Civil War

Oliver Cromwell

10 of May the Boocke of Spartes upon the Lords day was burnt by the Hangman in the place where the Crosse stoode, & at Exchange

Puritans burning a book of which they did not approve

At first it seemed as if the Cavaliers, led by Prince Rupert, would be victorious. But Cromwell trained his army of Puritan Ironsides and defeated the Royalists in two decisive battles. King Charles was brought to trial and condemned to death. He was executed in front of Whitehall Palace in 1649. Cromwell later became Lord Protector and ruled the country until his death in 1658. He always refused to become king.

Cromwell was a great man who loved his country, but he was a dictator. His followers, the Puritans, believed that pleasure was wicked, so theatres were shut and laws were made against betting, Sunday games, music, dancing and even singing.

The people as a whole did not like these restrictions and they joyfully welcomed Charles II back from exile. Charles was easy-going and fond of pleasure; he encouraged science, sport, music, art and acting.

Charles II

49

A red cross was painted on house doors where the plague had struck

Samuel Pepys

There were several disasters in the reign of Charles II. In 1665, a hot summer and the filthy streets caused a fever known as the Plague, or the Pestilence, to spread quickly, and thousands of Londoners died. A man named Samuel Pepys kept a secret diary at this time, written in shorthand. Here are some of the things he wrote down:

June 7th. This day I did in Drury Lane see two or three houses marked with a red cross upon the doors and 'Lord have mercy upon us' writ there, which was a sad sight to me.

June 21st. I find all the town almost going out of town, the coaches and waggons being all full of people going into the country.

People who were ill with the plague were taken away in closed litters or coaches to a kind of hospital known as a pest-house. At night men with carts collected the dead.

The dead were taken outside the walls and buried in the fields

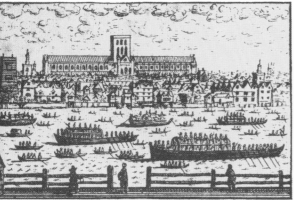

People left the City in boats

The churchyards were full

> Lord! how sad a sight it is to see the streets empty of people and two shops out of three, if not more, shut up.

One day, Pepys saw a naked child being passed out of the window of a house:

> It was the child of a citizen in Gracious Street, a saddler, who had buried all the rest of his children of the plague, and he and his wife being now shut up in despair of escaping, did desire only to save the life of this little child; and so prevailed to have it received, stark naked into the arms of a friend, who brought it, having put it into new fresh clothes, to Greenwich; where, upon hearing the story, we did agree it should be permitted to be received and kept in the town.

When the winter came, the plague grew less, but next year, 1666, another disaster happened: The Great Fire of London.

A corpse bearer

A funeral procession

Returning after the plague

The Great Fire of London

Samuel Pepys wrote in his Diary:

September 2nd. Jane called us up about 3 in the morning, to tell us of a great fire they saw in the City. So I rose and slipped on my nightgown and went to her window . . . By and by, Jane comes and tells us that she hears that above 300 houses have been burned down by the fire and that it is now burning down all Fish Street.

. . . so down, with heart full of trouble, to the Lieutenant of the Tower, who tells me that it began this morning in the King's baker's house in Pudding Lane . . . So I down to the waterside, everybody endeavouring to remove their goods and flinging them into the river . . .

. . . poor people staying in their houses as long as till the very fire touched them, and then running into boats or clambering from one pair of stairs by the waterside, to another . . .

Having seen the fire rage every way and nobody endeavouring to quench it, I to Whitehall in my boat and did tell the King and the Duke of York what I saw . . . the King command me to go to my Lord Mayor and command him to spare no house. . . .

Fire buckets and a squirt

At last I met my Lord Mayor and to the King's message he cried like a fainting woman, 'Lord, what can I do? I am spent. People will not obey me. I have been pulling down houses but the fire overtakes us faster than we can do it.'

That night Pepys 'saw the fire as one entire arch of fire above a mile long: it made me weep to see it. The churches, houses and all on fire and flaming at once, and a horrid noise the flames made and the cracking of the houses.'

The next day, Samuel buried his wine, a great cheese and other valuables in a hole in the garden. By nightfall the fire had reached the bottom of the garden. Carrying his bag of gold, he took his wife and their maid Jane down the river in a boat to safety. Fortunately, his house escaped, though he saw 'all the town burned and a miserable sight of Paul's Church with all the roofs fallen.'

Attempts were made to check the fire by pulling down houses in its path, but finally parties of sailors blew up houses with gunpowder, to make wide gaps which the flames could not pass. The Great Fire had burned down 84 churches, including old St Paul's, many fine wooden buildings and hundreds of wooden houses, which were built close together. It destroyed the filthy alleys and narrow streets of London, cleansing the town of all traces of the plague. But the worst slums, outside the walls, were untouched by the fire.

Old St Paul's, which was destroyed by the fire. Notice the windmill on the left

Refugees arrive in the country

A church built by Wren

After the fire

In six years London was rebuilt, and Sir Christopher Wren, the famous architect, designed St Paul's Cathedral and many other beautiful churches. He made a splendid plan for a new London with fine wide streets and noble buildings, but people would not follow it. They mostly rebuilt their houses where they had been before.

The new houses were built of brick and stone instead of wood, and seemed so handsome that everyone who could afford to, built himself one. The streets became cleaner and a little straighter.

Below is an artist's impression of the new St Paul's Cathedral, which was built after the Great Fire. You can see that it is very different from the first St Paul's.

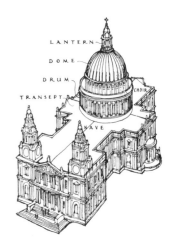

Sir Christopher Wren, the new St Paul's and Wren's plan for rebuilding London which was never carried out

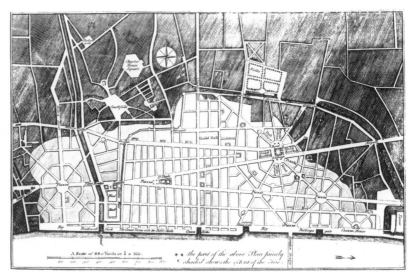

A third disaster in Charles II's reign was the war with Holland, when the Dutch sailed up the river Medway and burned the towns of Chatham and Rochester. Parliament was distressed at this happening, and spent money on new ships for the Navy. Not long afterwards the British Navy defeated the Dutch at sea. Samuel Pepys was one of the men who were responsible for improving the Navy.

The 'Royal James' burning during a battle with the Dutch in 1672

James II

William and Mary

Queen Anne

James II, Charles's brother, was the next king. He did not rule wisely, and when he tried to make England a Catholic country, he became very unpopular. After only three years, he was driven into exile by the 'Glorious Revolution' and his daughter Mary and her Dutch husband William of Orange became king and queen, as William III and Mary.

The last of the Stuarts was Queen Anne, the second daughter of James II. She was a good-natured woman and very religious, but she was dull and always ready to be guided by others. Because of this weakness, she was completely ruled for many years by John Churchill, Duke of Marlborough, and his wife Sarah, her closest friend.

The Duke of Marlborough was a famous soldier, and he won several great victories over the French. One of the most important was the Battle of Blenheim.

There were some great writers in Stuart times: John Milton, the Puritan poet of Cromwell's day, Robert Herrick, a Cavalier poet, John Bunyan, the author of *Pilgrim's Progress,* John Donne, the poet who became Dean of St Paul's, and John Webster, whose melodramatic tragedies are still acted. Many plays of Charles II's time are also still performed.

Blenheim Palace

Homes and Travel in Stuart Times 6

Homes

Before Stuart times men planned their own homes, but now there were architects, whose job was to design buildings and churches. Inigo Jones was the first important architect. He designed some fine buildings for James I and Charles I, such as the Banqueting Hall, which can still be seen in Whitehall. He started a new fashion in building, for he had travelled in Italy, where he saw new houses being built in the style of the ancient Roman temples.

After the Great Fire, Sir Christopher Wren built large houses and many churches, using Inigo Jones's style, but improving upon it.

Inigo Jones, the first important British architect

Hampton Court, the Tudor palace on the left and Wren's building on the right

The Queen's House at Greenwich designed by Inigo Jones

A Jacobean room. Notice the fine ceiling and the carving of the fireplace and table legs

A picture frame probably carved by Grinling Gibbons

The new houses were not built with a timber frame like Tudor homes, but were made of stone and brick, flat-fronted with pillars and handsome windows in what is called the classical style. The hall was no longer the chief room, but only an entrance place.

Rooms were big and high, with patterns and pictures on the ceilings. The walls were covered with wooden panelling called wainscoting. Doors, staircases and furniture were wonderfully carved.

Grinling Gibbons, one of the world's finest wood-carvers, lived at this time. He often worked for Christopher Wren and did much of the carving in St Paul's Cathedral.

Furniture

Furniture became more comfortable in Stuart times. Chairs began to have leather backs and padded seats, or even silk upholstery, but armchairs were still very rare. Besides oak, walnut was used in furniture-making. Walnut is less hard than oak, and this led to much decoration and carving. Wooden chests now had two drawers in the bottom, and later they became 'a chest of drawers'.

Well-to-do folk began to put leather carpets on the floor in place of rushes. Beds became very tall and costly, and had elaborate hangings, often in velvet brocade.

Samuel Pepys always pulled his bed-curtains, except once, during the Great Fire. 'I home late to Sir W Penn's, who did give me a bed, but without curtains . . . so here I went the first time into a naked bed.'

Fashionable people had their portraits painted, and hung them on their walls with other pictures and looking-glasses.

A chair made of walnut

The state bedroom at Chatsworth, Derbyshire, built in the 1680s

A four-poster bed

59

A clock made about 1670

At night, the rooms were lit by candles, but as they were very dear, ordinary people could not afford them. They went to bed early and began work at dawn. Glass was now quite common; windows became larger and were opened by pushing up the lower half.

Wood, which began to get scarce in Tudor times, was not plentiful, particularly in London, so fireplaces were made smaller, to take 'sea-coal'. This came from Newcastle by sea and was sold in the streets. People grumbled about the smoke and the dirt which it made in their fine new homes.

Fires and candles were difficult to light, since there were no boxes of matches like those of today. Instead, every house had a 'tinder box', a round iron box, with tinder (scorched rag) in it, a flint, a piece of steel and a little stick of wood dipped in sulphur.

The flint and steel were rubbed together until a spark set the tinder aglow. The sulphur match was then pushed into the glow and burst into flame, and the fire or candle was lit from this match. A round lid, called the damper, was pressed on the glowing tinder to put it out.

A flat-iron. A piece of heated metal was placed inside

Using a tinder box

Food

Meals were much the same as in Tudor times. Breakfast was now more satisfying: cold meat, perhaps, with oatcake and beer. A workman might have bread, radishes and ale.

Dinner was eaten about 12 o'clock and lasted a long time. There was no such meal yet as 'tea', but supper came at 5 or 6 o'clock, when the food was much the same as at breakfast.

Food was cooked over an open fire in pots, and joints of meat or birds were roasted on long spits, turned round and round by a little dog running inside a wheel. Although potatoes and salads were becoming popular, everyone still ate far more meat than is eaten today. The ration for sailors was two pounds of meat every day! When a man gave a dinner-party he often had the food cooked at a cook-shop, and carried through the streets to his house by the server in his white cap and apron.

A kitchen in Stuart times

Many people in Stuart times played musical instruments

Table forks

Samuel Pepys tells us of a 'pretty dinner' when they had 'a brace of stewed carp, six roasted chickens, a jowle of salmon, a tanzy (a dish of eggs and cream), two neat's tongues (ox-tongues) and cheese.'

Goose pie was a favourite dish, so were buttered shrimps, or pigeons stuffed with gooseberries. Other strange dishes were boiled grapes in butter, dates in soup, oysters stewed in wine, and snails.

After dinner, it was the custom to play games, to sing and to dance. Guests who came to dinner brought their own spoons and perhaps one of the new French forks. It was considered polite to keep your hat on when eating, but to raise it to your neighbour when you drank his health.

People drank a great deal and were often 'merry', which was a polite way of saying 'drunk'. There were strange drinks: *syllabub,* a sweet wine with cream, *mum,* a beer brewed from wheat, *buttered ale,* served hot and flavoured with cinnamon and butter, and *raspberry sack,* a sweet wine.

From the East came *tea, cocoa* (or chocolate) and *coffee,* which led to the opening of coffee-houses, where men went to chat and to smoke their clay pipes. Tea, or 'tay', was expensive at first, and cost fifty shillings a pound, but it became cheaper and more popular when the Court ladies made it the fashionable drink.

The Vertue of the *COFFEE* Drink.

First publiquely made and sold in England, by *Pasqua Rosee.*

THE Grain or Berry called *Coffee,* groweth upon little Trees, only in the *Deserts of Arabia.*

It is brought from thence, and drunk generally throughout all the Grand Seigniors Dominions.

It is a simple innocent thing, composed into a Drink, by being dryed in an Oven, and ground to Powder, and boiled up with Spring water, and about half a pint of it to be drunk, fasting an hour before, and not Eating an hour after, and to be taken as hot as possibly can be endured; the which will never fetch the skin off the mouth, or raise any Blisters, by reason of that Heat.

The Turks drink at meals and other times, is usually *Water,* and their Dyet consist much of *Fruit,* the Crudities whereof are very much corrected by this Drink.

The quality of this Drink is cold and Dry; and though it be a Dryer, yet it neither *heats,* nor *inflames* more then hot *Posset.*

It so closeth the Orifice of the Stomack, and fortifies the heat within; it's very good to help digestion, and therefore of great use to be about 3 or 4 a Clock afternoon, as well as in the morning.

uccn quickens the *Spirits,* and makes the Heart *Lightsome.*

is good against sore Eys, and the better if you hold your Head over it, and take in the Steem that way.

It suppresseth Fumes exceedingly, and therefore good against the *Head-ach,* and will very much stop any *Defluxion of Rheums,* that distil from the *Head* upon the *Stomack,* and so prevent and help *Consumptions;* and the *Cough of the Lungs.*

It is excellent to prevent and cure the *Dropsy, Gout,* and *Scurvy.*

It is known by experience to be better then any other Drying Drink for *People in years,* or *Children* that have any *running humors* upon them, as *the Kings Evil.* &c.

It is very good to prevent *Mis-carryings in Child-bearing Women.*

It is a most excellent Remedy against the *Spleen, Hypocondriack Winds,* or the like.

It will prevent *Drowsiness,* and make one fit for busines, if one have occasion to *Watch;* and therefore you are not to Drink of it after Supper, unless you intend to be *watchful,* for it will hinder sleep for 3 or 4 hours.

It is observed that in Turkey, *where this is generally drunk, that they are not troubled with the Stone, Gout, Dropsie, or Scurvey, and that their Skins are exceeding cleer and white.*

It is neither *Laxative* nor *Restringent.*

Made and Sold in St. *Michaels Alley* in *Cornhill,* by Pasqua Rosee, at the Signe of his own Head.

An advertisement for coffee

A coffee house

Poor people's homes

These were still draughty little huts made of clay and small stones, or wooden boards tarred with pitch.

A weaver working in his cottage

As the Government put a tax on chimneys to raise money, the poor had to manage without them and let the smoke find its way out of the roof-hole. A house with more than six windows was also taxed, but peasants were fortunate if they had even one glass window. Instead of glass, they used paper soaked in oil, which let in a little light.

Homes at this time were often workshops. The weaver had his loom in the cottage and his wife and children all helped in spinning and combing the wool. Craftsmen, like tailors, silversmiths, clockmakers, saddlers and glovers worked in their own homes.

Making oatcakes in a Yorkshire cottage. The picture was drawn about 1800, but little had changed in this time

a Porter

A blacksmith

A wheelwright

a Chilt~en-man

a Box-maker

Making paper

Dyeing cloth

a Button-maker

Although there were no real factories, work-places for such trades as glass-blowing, printing and the new silk-making, steadily grew bigger. Coal-mining and iron smelting were becoming important in the North of England, and the brewers, dyers and soap-makers were said to make 'a horrid smoke' in London.

A sedan chair

Travel in Stuart times

Although the roads were very bad and dangerous, more and more people made journeys about the country, for trade and even for pleasure. They usually travelled on horseback or on foot, while merchants sent their goods by pack-horse or in heavy stage-waggons, which were even slower than the barges on the rivers.

The picture below shows a royal procession passing through Cheapside, London, in Stuart times. It was drawn by an artist of the time. He has made the street look much wider than it really was, so that he could include the two coaches, a horse-litter and a large number of soldiers.

In London, the latest way of going about was by hackney coaches, which could be hired for a shilling a mile. They were useful for rich people, whose fine clothes would be spoiled if they walked in the muddy streets, crowded with carts, workmen, stalls and passers-by.

Cheapside, about 1630

Sedan chairs were popular, for they took up less room in the narrow streets; there were private chairs, and others for hire. At first they had curtains, but soon they were fitted with glass windows, like the coaches.

A hackney coach

The carriers and waggoners acted as postmen, taking letters (and messages for people who could not write) as well as parcels, from town to town. Charles I started the Royal Mails, which were carried by postboys riding along the main roads. The person who received a letter had to pay for it. It cost twopence for a sheet of paper, and as there were no envelopes, the paper was folded and sealed with a blob of wax.

Stage-coaches probably started in Cromwell's time. They ran on certain days from London to large towns like York (8 days), Bath (3 days) and Exeter (8 days). The passengers slept each night at an inn in a different town. Sometimes in winter the roads were too bad for coach travel.

A postboy

A cart in the London streets

A running footman

With the stage-coaches came a new danger: the highwayman. He worked alone, instead of with a gang of robbers. He knew when to expect the coach, and chose a wooded spot on a hill where it was easy to hold it up at the point of a pistol. These highwaymen, called 'tobymen', were often well-known characters, with friends at the inns on the main roads.

In Charles II's reign the nobility had 'flying chariots' which would travel over 100 kilometres a day. These fine coaches were accompanied by servants on horseback. The servants protected them against robbers, pulled the coach out of deep ruts, or mended a wheel when it came off, which was quite a common happening. Some noblemen even sent running footmen ahead of them to clear the way. These footmen carried a long staff, which had a little bowl at one end filled with drink to quench their thirst.

Outside an Oxford college, 1674

When he had become quite rich, Pepys tells us that he went to choose 'a little chariot' which was painted silver and had gilt windows. He also tells us of a flying chariot made of wicker, so that it would be very light, but it did not travel as fast as his friend boasted.

With all this traffic the roads became worse, until a way was found to raise money for mending them. Toll-gates were built at which travellers were stopped and made to pay a sum of money towards the cost of repairs. When riders began to dash past without paying, a law was made that a road could be blocked by a turnpike, a gate with spikes. The main roads were gradually improved with the money paid by travellers.

An early fire engine

These Engins (which are ... the best) to quinch great Fires; are

JOHN KEELING

A hired boat before London Bridge

A royal barge

Boats and ships

Because the streets were narrow and crowded, the river Thames was London's chief highway in Tudor and Stuart times. Boats of every kind, carrying goods and passengers, went up and down the river all day and even at night, when they were lit by lanterns.

There were gilded barges of the King and Queen and the great nobles, small boats and wherries, merchant ships and slow barges laden with coal and grain, light skiffs with one passenger, bum-boats and racing hoys.

Pepys himself was often going up and down the river to Whitehall, Woolwich and Greenwich. Once he saw 'the King and Queen in a barge under a canopy, with 1000 barges and boats with them.'

All along the river there was bustle, with boatmen and traders at work. There were stone steps at many places, where folk could hire a boat from the fierce and quarrelsome watermen, who bawled out jokes and rude remarks to every boat that passed by. Queen Elizabeth's favourite palace was at Greenwich and she was often to be seen in her royal barge as she travelled from Whitehall.

Charles II was a keen sailor and he started a new fashion by having a yacht built for racing; 'a pretty thing', says Pepys, and supposed to be faster than the Dutch yachts.

A Thames waterfront

Small sailing boats like this carried goods round the coast

The old palace at Greenwich. Queen Elizabeth frequently came down the river in her barge

*An English naval
squadron at sea*

After Elizabeth's reign the Navy grew weaker. James I and
Parliament would not spare the money to build new ships,
but Charles I ordered the great *Sovereign of the Seas* (later
called *Royal Sovereign*), which was far bigger than Drake's
ships and carried more sail.

Cromwell and Charles II had new warships built to fight
against the Dutch, for this was a time of naval warfare.
There were also sea-battles with the French in William III's
and Anne's reigns. Conditions in the Navy were disgraceful; the sailors were badly treated and often had no pay, but
the men and their admirals showed the same skill and
bravery as in Elizabeth's day.

*The 'Britannia', with a
yacht on the right*

London in Samuel Pepys's Time 7

The streets

There was still a high wall round the city of London in Charles II's reign, but houses spread into the fields to the east, northwards and down towards the palace of Whitehall.

The narrow cobbled streets were very noisy and full of people, carts and coaches. Everyone shouted out his trade and the goods which he had to sell. The apprentices outside their masters' shops bawled, 'What d'ye lack?' and the street-sellers cried their wares: 'Sweet lavender,' 'Cherry ripe,' 'Lilywhite vinegar,' 'Any milk, here,' 'Any brass pots, iron pots, skillets or frying-pans to mend?'

There were sellers of eggs, cakes, rabbits, mouse-traps and ginger-bread; there were coalmen with sacks of Newcastle sea-coal on their backs, custard-mongers, apple-hawkers and rag-pickers, all bawling their loudest. There were wandering tradesmen, such as tinkers, chair-menders, rat-catchers, old-clothes men and basket-makers, and they all roared their loudest, 'Buy! Buy! Buy!' in the muddy, cobbled streets.

A ballad singer

'Rats or mice to kill?'

'Sausages!'

Street traders cried their wares

Half the things now sold in shops were then hawked in the streets or sold in the markets, such as Cheapside, Poultry and Fish Wharf.

The coaches, sedan chairs and waggons would get jammed, wheels would come off and fights break out. Everyone shouted and joined in, and often people were killed.

The streets of Samuel Pepys's time also had many unpleasant smells. An open gutter ran down the middle of each street and everyone threw rubbish, stable-manure, slops and dirty water into the gutter or a nearby corner.

There were many horses, and how to get rid of stable manure was a real problem. At one time, there were as many as seven hundred hackney coaches for hire, and other horses for riding, for private carriages, waggons and drays.

The Gresham steelyard, a form of weighing machine

A London square

74

Drinking in a tavern

As there were no drain-pipes, rain-water gushed from the roofs into the streets. Servants thought nothing of opening an upstairs window and flinging dirty water into the street, sometimes on to an unlucky passer-by. It is not surprising that fevers and plague came to the city nearly every year. Fortunately, the Plague of 1665 was the last serious outbreak.

Taverns, eating-houses and cook-shops were plentiful. The finest taverns were *Locket's* at Charing Cross and *The Dolphin,* where Pepys often went for a good dinner. Most people took the 'ordinary' at an inn or tavern. This was dinner eaten with all the other guests at a long table, and cost a shilling or eighteen pence.

Wealthier folk ordered a special meal in another room, and sent their own servants to the kitchen to see that it was cooked to their liking. Some of these servants were as proud and haughty as their masters. Humbler folk took their meals in the kitchen.

In the taverns, wine shops and the new coffee-houses men sat, smoked, and talked about serious matters as well as the latest gossip.

London streets before the Fire

75

A duel

The quarrelsome Londoners

People seem to have been very quarrelsome. The butchers and weavers, for instance, were always attacking each other. Duels were often fought by the rich and fights broke out every day in the streets. Only gentlemen were supposed to carry swords; ordinary men carried clubs and daggers.

If two waggoners met in a narrow street, neither would give way, but both leapt down and started a furious battle. Two strangers, walking close to the wall to keep out of puddles would draw their swords rather than move aside. If a man was jostled by another he would knock him into the gutter. There were no policemen to keep order in those days.

As we shall see later, punishments were dreadful, and flogging was common. Fathers flogged their children, masters whipped their apprentices and officers flogged rogues, soldiers and sailors. No wonder people were fierce and quarrelsome.

The fiercest of all were the watermen, who rowed passengers on the river. They fought each other and often their passengers too. They were so strong in numbers and so fierce that they prevented the building of bridges over the Thames, as this might take away their trade.

Thus, at this time, there was still only one bridge over the river: the famous London Bridge, with its double row of houses and shops and even a chapel.

Whipping at the cart's tail

76

The London mob

Very much feared in these days by kings, lords and citizens was the London mob, crowds of rough men and women who would quickly collect whenever there was any excitement, or an event which pleased or angered them. They would march through the streets in a riot, attacking whoever displeased them, burning and damaging houses, until the soldiers were called out to restore order. Although they were unruly, their actions sometimes prevented the King and nobles from behaving like dictators.

When Charles II was welcomed, the mob joyfully lit bonfires in the streets, broke the windows of Puritans' houses, roasted great joints of beef and made every passer-by kneel down to drink the King's health.

The apprentice lads were just as unruly, and although there were many laws to prevent their misbehaviour, they constantly took part in fighting and rioting. On one occasion five hundred apprentices tried to burn down the Archbishop of Canterbury's palace.

The London mob

THE BELMAN
OF LONDON.
Bringing to light the most notorious
villanies that are now practised
in the KINGDOME.

Profitable for Gentlemen, Lawyers, Merchants, Citizens, Farmers,
Masters of Houshold, and all sorts of servants, to marke,
and delightfull for all men to Reade,

Lege, Perlege, Relege.

Printed at London for NATHANIEL BVTTER. 1 6 0 8.

A watchman, 1608

The streets at night

The streets were dark and dangerous at night, and all good citizens stayed at home. There were a few lanterns hung at corners, but people who were out late usually hired a link-boy with a torch or lantern to light them home, or their servants walked in front with a light.

A few old watchmen, known as *Charlies,* roamed the streets at night, carrying a staff and lantern, and sometimes a bell. They called out the time in each street, 'Past twelve o'clock, and a fine frosty night!'

Thieves, cut-purses and footpads waited in the alleys and would even rob coaches and sedan chairs. The feeble old watchmen usually took good care to keep out of the way when there was any trouble of this kind.

'Charlies' arresting a drunk

Executions

This was a cruel time, and great crowds gathered to watch executions and punishments in the open-air. Gentlefolk were beheaded, and it was at least a quick death. Ordinary criminals were dragged through the streets on a hurdle, or whipped behind a cart. They were then hanged and their bodies were cut in four.

The bodies of thieves and highwaymen were left hanging in iron frames on the gibbet, and the heads of traitors were still occasionally placed on spikes on London Bridge.

The heads of executed traitors had been put on spikes on the gate of London Bridge

Witches were tried with very rough justice

A witch, the devil, and the witch's 'familiar'

Witches

Everyone, the great, the wise and the learned, believed in witches.

James I even wrote a book about them. Witch-hunting was widespread and any poor old woman who lived alone with her cat was likely to be blamed for accidents or bad luck. She might be accused of being a witch, of flying on her broomstick and of weaving spells. She was tortured until she confessed, after which she was burned alive or hanged. She might be flung, bound, into the river; if she sank she was innocent, but if she floated, she was guilty.

Between 1603 and 1683, it is said that 70 000 persons were put to death for witchcraft, many of them by Matthew Hopkins, the Witchfinder General of the Civil War.

The theatre

The theatres, closed by the Puritans, opened again when Charles II came to the throne. *The Globe* and *The Fortune* had been destroyed and the chief theatres were now the *King's Theatre* in Drury Lane, and the *Duke of York's*. After such a long period without plays, the people became very fond of theatre-going.

The theatres were small and more comfortable than before, and the pit was no longer open to the sky, but had a ceiling or covering of some kind. The seats were expensive: a box cost four shillings, a seat in the pit was half a crown, and in the gallery a shilling. These prices must be multiplied by about thirty to get some idea of their value today.

Plays were acted in the afternoons, chiefly because the stage could not be well lit at night. In those days everyone arose very early and did most of their work in the morning.

In the theatre women's parts were now taken by the actresses instead of by boys, and it was the fashion for ladies in the audience to wear masks, since there was still a feeling that the theatre was not a very nice place in which to be seen.

Theatres were opened again after the Restoration

81

Hawking was a sport still enjoyed in the country

At Court, masques were popular. They were partly acted and partly mimed, and included music and dancing. They were often staged at night on the river, with beautiful lighting effects.

The poorer people found their entertainment at *The Red Bull* at Clerkenwell and at *The Bear and Bull Gardens,* where dogs fought bears and bulls. This sport was beginning to die out. They still enjoyed cock-fights, laying bets that one bird would kill the other.

In his diary Pepys writes: 'I did go to Shoe Lane to see a cock-fighting at a new pit, but, Lord, to see the strange variety of people, from Parliament-men to the poorest prentices, bakers, butchers, brewers, draymen and whatnot —strange to observe the nature of these poor birds how they will fight till they drop down dead on the table.'

At the great Bartholomew Fair on Midsummer Eve, they watched wrestling, rope-dancers, acrobats and trained apes doing tricks. On May-day Pepys saw the milkmaids dance down the Strand, with flowers and silver-edged buckets, for even if it was a rough and cruel age, the people knew how to enjoy themselves.

Bear-baiting

Actors at the Red Bull playhouse

Hunting the hare was a sport for gentlemen

Games

The Puritans forbade games after church on Sundays. They publicly burned James I's *Book of Sports* in which he set down the sports which could be played after church. When Charles II came to the throne sports were again allowed. The King himself, the 'merry monarch', was a keen tennis-player, yachtsman and huntsman. He also started horse-racing at Newmarket, and this led to the new sport of fox-hunting.

Real (that is, Royal) Tennis

Horseracing at Windsor, with King Charles II in the stand

Angling was popular at this time

Several new games appeared at this time. Pell-mell was played by the King and his courtiers in St James's Park. Golf, which had been played in Holland and Scotland for many years, now became a fashionable game in England. Boxing, fencing, fishing and skating were popular, and even bell-ringing became a sport.

It is thought that cricket started about this time, perhaps by throwing a ball at a three-legged milking stool, while the batsman tried to hit the ball away with a thick stick.

The old Tudor sports came back again: bowls and skittles in the inn-gardens, quoits, cudgels, wrestling and football, which was still played in the streets and on the commons, with any number of players on each side, and without rules or referee!

In the winter evenings, people played chess, draughts, billiards, dominoes, cribbage, dice and cards. Music and dancing were other favourite indoor pastimes.

The new game of pell-mell

Pleasure places

Bathing at Bath

Besides the theatres and the bear gardens, the taverns and the coffee-houses, Londoners now had parks in which they could enjoy themselves. Hyde Park had always been a royal hunting-ground, but in Cromwell's time coaches were allowed to drive in it, and carriage races were held there. During Charles II's reign it was opened to the general public, as it is today.

Hyde Park, where fashionable people went to gossip and be seen

The nave of old St Paul's Cathedral

Vauxhall Gardens

St James's Park and the Mulberry Gardens were fashionable places for a stroll. The Mulberry Gardens were planted for the silkworm industry, and were in the place where Buckingham Palace now stands. Vauxhall Gardens was another favourite place for amusement where the citizens enjoyed music, as well as cheese-cakes, syllabub and wine.

Strangely enough, the fashionable place for the young gallants to show off their fine clothes was in the nave of old St Paul's Cathedral. They strolled up and down and chatted to their friends.

Covent Garden and the Royal Exchange were other places where these idle and often wicked young men could be seen lounging and swaggering. Inigo Jones laid out Covent Garden with gardens and covered arches or piazzas where people could stroll. This became the centre of London's night-life and, by day, a fruit and vegetable market.

People in Stuart Times 8

A horn-book

Children

As you can see from the picture below, children were usually dressed like grown-ups. Notice their large feathered hats. They had to be very polite to their parents, for fathers thought it was their duty to beat them. Pepys was really a kind-hearted man, but he sometimes beat and kicked his servants, and once he beat his little servant girl and shut her up all night in the cellar.

Most children did not go to school at all. Boys learned their father's trade, or were made apprentices, and most grew up without ever needing to read and write. Girls usually became servants, lady's-maids or sempstresses, sewing clothes for gentlefolk.

Lessons started early in life for children of the well-to-do. They learned to read from horn-books, which were like little wooden bats, with the alphabet carved or pasted on. Often they were covered with a thin sheet of horn and cost three pence each. Children practised writing on slates and later used goose-quills and paper.

The children of King Charles I

A bookshop

The boys went to Grammar School when they were old enough, and learned Latin, Greek, scripture and grammar, but very little arithmetic. When Pepys was grown up, and quite an important man, he started to learn his multiplication tables. He writes that he was 'up by four o'clock and at my multiplication table hard, which is all the trouble I meet with in my arithmetique.'

Such schools as Winchester, Eton, St Paul's and Westminster, were already famous, but, like the other Grammar Schools of the time, were usually only for sons of merchants, the gentry and squires.

Books could be bought in Paternoster Row, a narrow street close to St Paul's Cathedral. They were very expensive and much prized. Boys had few school books, and most of their lessons were learnt by heart from their teacher.

Girls learnt needlework, deportment (how to walk and behave themselves in company), dancing, cookery and household management. It was rare to find a woman who understood Latin and Greek as Queen Elizabeth did.

88

Clothes

Fashions changed considerably in Stuart times. The cavaliers dressed richly but the Elizabethan ruff disappeared and large lace collars were worn instead.

The huge trunks were no longer padded, but became loose trousers which were fastened to a coat. These trousers, or breeches, were either secured at the knee with ribbons or went into wide leather boots. The men's hair was long and curled, and some wore earrings and rouge.

Ladies' skirts were no longer worn over a farthingale, as they were in Elizabeth's day, but were high-waisted and often looped up. They were made of stiff silk and satin, with fine petticoats, and lace was used wherever possible.

This was the century of lace. Court ladies wore two or three pairs of gloves at once. They carried muffs, fans and masks. Veils, pearls and furs were the height of fashion.

Court dress in the cavalier period

A merchant's wife, about 1640, and a cavalier

The Puritans thought it was wicked to wear rich and brightly coloured clothes, so they dressed in plain, dark garments, with white collars and aprons. It was vanity to have long curled hair, so they cut theirs short.

A Puritan family

When Charles II came back to the throne, elaborate clothes in the gayest of colours were again in fashion, for men as well as for women.

Pepys bought his wife a green petticoat of flowered satin with fine black and white lace for £5 (a huge sum of money), a slashed waistcoat and a yellow hood.

A lace collar

90

Men's dress was as gay or gayer than the ladies'. Pepys was forever buying new clothes. One day he dressed himself in a velvet cloak, a silk suit and coat trimmed with gold buttons and gold lace at the wrists. Waistcoats, silk stockings and shoes with fancy buckles were the latest fashion, and the gallants spent large sums of money on these extravagances.

Gentlemen now wore long curled wigs, and had thin moustaches like the King's. Beards went out of fashion. Mr Pepys visited his barber once or twice a week for a shave. On other days he rubbed his face with a pumice stone.

Men of fashion wore swords and carried muffs and looking-glasses. Taking snuff from a little silver box, with an elegant twirl of the fingers, was the latest habit.

It was only the rich who dressed in these bright and expensive clothes. The country folk and poor townspeople wove their own cloth and made their own simple garments. Women wore woollen dresses and red petticoats. Men wore breeches of thick wool or thin leather. Craftsmen wore aprons of different colours: grocers a white apron, brewers blue, blacksmiths a leather one, while butchers dressed in blue, and footmen in white.

A fashionable woman wearing a mask

A muff

A barber's shop

The gentry liked to dress their servants as richly as possible and provided uniforms, called livery, in the family colour.

The merchants and well-to-do citizens dressed better than the workmen, but less richly than the gentlefolk.

At the end of the Stuart Age a lady and gentleman dressed like this. Notice his three-cornered hat, huge cuffs and flared embroidered coat. Every lady of fashion carried a fan.

Countrywoman, 1600

Tradesman's wife, 1650

Citizen's daughter, 1650

Common folk did not wear underclothes at all, but fine ladies wore vests and petticoats. Nightdresses were worn by ladies, but nightgowns or pyjamas were unknown for men. They went to bed in a shirt or nothing at all. The nightgown which Pepys put on while watching the Great Fire was probably some kind of loose robe.

This age of elegance was a time of fine manners and great courtesy. Raising their plumed hats, gentlemen bowed low to ladies and kissed their hands. They even greeted each other in this way. Kissing was very popular with everyone and it was a much more common greeting than shaking hands.

Gentleman and woman, 1610   *Countryman and woman, 1610*

Samuel Pepys in later life. His wig would have cost about £2

Prices

It is interesting to compare the prices of some articles about which we have been reading with those of today. To do this, the prices must be multiplied by twenty-five or thirty. Remember that until 1971, £1 was made up of 20 shillings with 12 pennies to the shilling.

A workman's wages were from 10 to 20 shillings a week, though often less.

meat 3d a pound	a hat £1
butter 6d a pound	a beaver hat £4 10s
cheese 2d a pound	shoes 4s a pair
beer ½d a bottle	silk stockings £1
claret wine 4s a gallon	gloves 15s
coat and breeches £8	a nightgown £5
lace collar and cuffs £3	a wig £2

Lady Howard, painted at the end of Queen Anne's reign

The end of the Stuart Age

When Queen Anne died in 1714 the throne went to George of Hanover, a German descendant of James I. George could hardly speak English, and he did not try to understand the English people. From this time onwards Parliament really ruled the country.

By the end of Queen Anne's reign life had become much more like the present time than it was in Henry VIII's reign. In warfare, gunpowder had caused the longbow and armour to disappear. At home, houses were made of brick and stone instead of wood and wattle.

Abroad, nearly all the world had been discovered and English traders had begun to travel to distant lands.

Meals were becoming different as new foods—potatoes, fruit, sugar, spices, tea and coffee—had been brought from across the seas. Men were now wearing jackets and breeches, instead of doublets, padded trunks and hose.

The king could no longer rule as he pleased. Parliament made the laws and saw that they were kept. Ordinary people had more rights and freedom than in former days.

Noble families were living in great magnificence. This is the
state dining room at Chatsworth House

Index

Looking at History   R J Unstead

Book Four

From Queen Anne
to Queen Victoria

Adam and Charles Black   London

Acknowledgements

Castle Museum, York   86d
Council of Industrial Design   75b, 85f, 86a & b
Cunard Ltd   67c
Derbyshire Countryside Ltd   26b, 27a, 30a
Mary Evans Picture Library   2, 4, 5c, 9a, b & c, 10b, 12b, 13a & b, 14a, 15a, 18b,
   19a, 23a, b & c, 24a & b, 25b, 31e, 32b & c, 33b & d, 34a, b & c, 35a, b & c, 36a,
   37a & b, 38a & c, 39a & c, 40a, 41a & b, 42a, 43a, 44b, 45a, 46a & b, 47b, 48b,
   49a, 51a, b, c & d, 52b & c, 54a & b, 55a, 56b, 57b, 58b, 59c & d, 60a, c & d, 62a,
   63b, 65a & d, 67a, 69a, 70b, c & d, 71a, b & c, 72a & b, 73b, 74c & e, 75a & c, 76d,
   77a, b & c, 78a, b & c, 79a & e, 80a & c, 81a, 82a & b, 83a & d, 84c & d, 85a, b, c,
   d, e & g, 86c, 87e, 88a & b, 89a & b, 90a, 92a & b, 93a, 94a & c, 95a, cover
Greater London Council   27b
Trustees of the London Museum   7a, 19b, 26a, 43b & c, 47a, 55b & c, 60b, 74d, 93b
London Transport   62b
Mansell Collection   1, 3, 5a & b, 6a, 10a, 11a & b, 16a, 18a, 20b, 25a, 28d, 29b,
   31a & b, 44a, 48a, 50b, 51e, 52a, 53a, b & c, 56a, 58a, 59a, 63c, 64a, 65b & c,
   66b & c, 68b, 73a, 76a & b, 91a, 95b
National Maritime Museum, London   20c, 21d, 22a & b, 23d, 67b, 68a, 70a
National Portrait Gallery   30b, 33c
Nineteenth Century Prints   61a
Pictorial Colour Slides   10c, 64b
Post Office   15b & c, 17a, 74a
Radio Times Hulton Picture Library   8a, 12a, 78d
Rothamsted Experimental Station   38d
Science Museum   57c, 61c
Trustees of the Tate Gallery   64c
Times Newspapers Ltd   50a
University of Reading, Museum of Rural Life   38b, 39b
A Vialls   74b
Victoria & Albert Museum   6b, 29a, 31c & d, 32a, 91b
P F White   28a, b & c, 69b, 83b & c, 84a & b
Robert Wood   58c, 59b, 61b
Woodmansterne Ltd & National Maritime Museum, London   20a, 21a, b & c
Illustrations 33a & e, 87a–d & f, 94b are from Iris Brooke's *English Costume of the
   Nineteenth Century*
Designed by Karen Bowen

Published by A & C Black Ltd
35 Bedford Row, London WC1R 4JH

ISBN 0 7136 1423 4 limp
   0 7136 1419 6 net
   0 7136 1572 9 complete edition of Books 1–5

First published 1974   Reprinted 1975 and 1977
© 1974 A & C Black Ltd. Also © 1953, 1961

Printed in Great Britain by Sir Joseph Causton & Sons Ltd
London and Eastleigh

Contents

Some People and Events in Georgian England 1

George II

George I (1714–1727) was a German relation of Queen Anne. He became King of the United Kingdom because the Catholic Stuarts were debarred from the throne. The next Kings were:

George II   (1727–1760)   George IV (1820–1830)
George III (1760–1820)   William IV (1830–1837)

The Jacobites and the 'Fifteen' and 'Forty-Five' Risings
In 1715, James II's son, James Edward, 'The Pretender,' tried to win back his father's throne but he failed dismally. His son, Bonnie Prince Charlie, made a bolder attempt in 1745, and frightened the English government by marching south as far as Derby. Eventually his Highlanders were utterly defeated at Culloden, and the Young Pretender, as he was called, escaped to France after many adventures.

John Wesley (1703–1791)
John Wesley, with his brother Charles Wesley, and George Whitefield, founded Methodism. They preached at great open-air meetings all over the country. John Wesley travelled 8000 kilometres a year, on foot and on horseback, for fifty years, bringing religion and happiness to countless people, especially poor and humble folk.

George III

War with France
The Seven Years' War with France lasted from 1757–1764. The year 1759 was known as the 'Year of Victories': James

The defeat of the Highlanders at Culloden, 1745

5

King William IV

The Duke of Wellington

Wolfe captured Quebec and added Canada to the British Empire, Admiral Hawke destroyed the French Fleet at Quiberon Bay and Robert Clive brought part of India under British rule.

The American Colonies

In George III's reign the settlers in America, who at this time had mostly come from Britain, objected to paying taxes to the 'home' country and declared their independence. Under the leadership of George Washington, and helped by the French, they defeated the British in 1781 and formed a new country, the United States of America.

The wars with Napoleon

After the French Revolution, which lasted from 1789–1793, the great general, Napoleon Bonaparte, led the French armies in their long struggle against Britain and her allies. Nelson's victory at Trafalgar (1805) saved England from invasion and gave her command of the seas. The Duke of Wellington wore down Napoleon's armies in Spain, and, with the Prussians under Blücher, defeated him finally at the battle of Waterloo (1815).

Reformers

The work of John Wesley led others to take an interest in the many poor and unfortunate people of these times. John Howard and Elizabeth Fry, both Quakers, worked hard to improve the crowded and unhealthy prisons, and to give prisoners a chance to lead better lives.

William Wilberforce made people realise that slavery was shameful, and through his work the Slave Trade, by which negroes had been carried off from their homes in Africa and sold in America, was stopped in 1807. Slavery was forbidden in British Dominions in 1833.

Lord Shaftesbury did much to help children and the poor. His Factory Acts gradually reduced the long hours worked by women and children in factories, and prevented them from going down the coalmines. Shaftesbury carried on his work into Queen Victoria's reign, starting the Ragged Schools, helping the poor and supporting a law to forbid small boys working as chimney-sweeps.

A guardsman, 1815

Travel in Georgian England 2

Roads

Travel became popular in Georgian times, but the dreadful condition of the roads and the likelihood of meeting high-waymen made it very dangerous.

Sometimes ruts in the roads became so deep that travellers were hidden from view, and there were pot-holes where a man might drown on a dark night. In some places the road disappeared altogether, and it was necessary to hire a guide to reach the next town. In wet weather travellers hired teams of oxen to drag their coach out of the mud, while in the summer the ruts were baked so hard that coaches sometimes turned off into the fields.

Each parish was supposed to look after its own roads, but little was done, and few people understood road-making. At last a plan was made to raise money to pay for repairs. Parliament allowed turnpikes and toll-gates on the busy roads, and travellers using the roads had to pay a toll, or fee, at each turnpike.

A turnpike on the outskirts of London

*Blind Jack of
Knaresborough*

Road-makers

The first of the new road-makers was John Metcalfe, known as Blind Jack of Knaresborough. He was given the job of laying 5 km of turnpike road in Yorkshire. He did it so well that he became a road-maker, and in time he laid over 300 km of road.

A more famous road-maker was Thomas Telford, a Scottish engineer. He realised that roads must be well drained. The foundation of his roads were dug deep, and filled with large stones, followed by layers of smaller stones, which were well rolled in. He built many roads, including the difficult Shrewsbury to Holyhead road. He also built the famous Menai Bridge.

Telford's methods were improved upon by John Macadam, another Scot, and the greatest road-maker of the time. Macadam said that deep digging and large stones were unnecessary. All that was needed was a layer, 10 to 12 inches deep, of small hard stones, not bigger than an inch long or wide. The iron-rimmed wheels of the coaches would grind a fine powder on top, which, washed down by rain, would bind the road together and keep it firm, but springy. People laughed at such a simple idea, until Macadam proved he was right.

He was then put in charge of road-making in many parts of the country, and by 1840, 35 000 km of new road had been laid, with 8000 turnpikes to pay for their upkeep. It was noticed that coach horses, which in the old days had been worn out after three years, now lasted seven years on these improved roads.

*Macadam building a
road*

An inn yard, with the stage-coach filling up

A landau

A barouche

The stage-coach

The most important vehicles on the new roads were the stage-coaches, which made regular runs between London and most large towns. They stopped at 'stages' along the road to put down and collect passengers, to change horses and to stay for the night at an inn.

The stage-coach was a heavy vehicle, pulled by four or six horses, and travelled at a steady 8 km/h. Inside the coach were two cushioned seats taking three persons on each side. Outside passengers travelled at a cheaper rate, either in the luggage basket which was slung between the back wheels, or on the roof, clinging to the baggage. It is difficult to say which was the more uncomfortable way of travelling.

About 1750, the coach which left London for Birmingham (177 km) took two and a half days over the journey. Dover (116 km) was a two-day journey, the passengers dining at Rochester and sleeping at Canterbury. Norwich was also two days' travelling distance, York was four and Exeter six. The long trip to Edinburgh (600 km) took ten days in summer and twelve in winter. The cost of so many meals and lodgings on the way made travel expensive.

Horses were changed about every 15 km at the 'stages', which were inns, each keeping a large number of horses for hire to the coach companies. While the horses were being changed in the yard, bustling with grooms, ostlers and post-boys, the passengers had a chance to stretch their legs. In winter they warmed their numbed fingers and took a glass of ale or steaming punch at the inn's fireside.

The arrival of a coach

A barouche (left) and a gig (right)

A post-chaise

A phaeton, now in a museum

Carriages

There were many other vehicles to be seen on the roads besides the stage-coaches. The *post-chaise* ('chaise' is pronounced 'shays') was lighter in build and faster than the stage-coach and had curved springs from which leather straps held the body. It was drawn by two or four horses, in charge of smart post-boys, who rode one to each pair of horses. Only well-to-do gentry could afford this way of travelling, which was considered to be much superior to travel by public stage-coach.

Lighter and faster still, was the *phaeton* ('fay-eton'), an open four-wheeled carriage drawn by one or two horses, which aristocratic travellers drove themselves.

A *gig* was a light two-wheeled cart pulled by one horse. A similar vehicle drawn by two horses was called a *curricle,* while a gig with a hood was a *cabriolet,* later known as a 'cab'. This gradually took the place of the heavy hackney-coach in London streets; its driver was known as a 'cabby'.

The *landau* (pronounced 'lando'), named after a German town, was a coach with a hood which could be opened. A *whiskey* was a light gig, and a *sulky* was the charming name given to a little carriage for one person only.

The stage-waggon

Strings of pack-horses laden with bundles of goods had not yet disappeared from the roads, and the huge stage-waggons, with their wide wheels and teams of eight and ten horses, continued to plod along at 4 or 5 km/h, to the annoyance of the coaches. Inside the waggons were as many as 30 or 40 passengers, who could not afford stage-coach prices. They sat huddled together on bales of merchandise.

The mail-coach

The finest of all the vehicles was the mail-coach. The first Royal Mail ran from Bath to London in 1784 and made the 170 km journey in the record time of 16 hours. As the roads improved, the mail-coach became the fastest vehicle of all, dashing along at a steady 19 km/h carrying passengers and the precious bags of letters. Behind rode the guard with his musical horn, and a blunderbuss for use against highwaymen. The mail-coach had a change of horses every 11 km, so that it could keep up its speed.

The mail-coach drivers were the lords of the road, well-dressed, and often young and handsome. They drove their splendid horses with superb skill, to the envy of every boy along the road.

A stage-waggon outside an inn

A whiskey

A cabriolet

11

Highwaymen

With coaches now travelling at greater speeds, and with the cutting down of trees bordering the roads, which had given shelter, it was more difficult for Tobymen to ply their trade, and they became less numerous. Another disadvantage for robbers was that travellers now began to carry paper money instead of gold, and this could be traced.

But there were still a few daring highwaymen who worked alone or in small groups, the most famous being Dick Turpin, really a horse-thief, who was hanged in 1739.

There was Captain Maclean, the Gentleman Highwayman, with his elegant manners and respectable friends, and Jack Rann, who had been a coachman. Jack Rann was known as 'Sixteen-string Jack' from his habit of wearing eight coloured laces at each knee of his breeches. He dressed in scarlet, with white silk stockings and laced hat. A bold and daring fellow, he boasted of his exploits. His boasting led to his downfall, and he was hanged at Newgate.

One famous hold-up took place in 1775, when the Norwich coach was waylaid in Epping Forest by seven highwaymen. The guard shot three of them dead with his blunderbuss before he was killed himself.

The fate of highwaymen—the gibbet

Lord Barrymore stopped by highwaymen in 1787

12

Horsemen

There were also many travellers who rode on horseback, from educated gentlemen who wished to see the countryside in their own way and at their own pace, to travelling pedlars on their bony hacks, taking ribbons, laces, combs and cotton goods into the villages. John Wesley, the great preacher, rode on horseback in all weathers, reading as he went.

If two companions had only one horse, they would journey in an amusing way called 'ride-and-tie'. One would start walking and the other would ride on ahead for some distance, when he would dismount, tie the horse to a tree and proceed on foot. Presently his friend would reach the horse, untie it, mount and ride on until he had passed his companion by several kilometres. He would then dismount, tether the horse and walk on.

Lastly, there were the poorest travellers, who made their way on foot, taking a lift on a stage-waggon when they could afford a few pence. These were the travelling players, jugglers, pedlars, journeymen and tinkers, and country lads trudging to London to seek their fortunes.

A clergyman setting out on a tour of the Lake District

13

*Stage-coach
passengers at breakfast*

The driver

Inns

The inns and posthouses in the towns and villages along the main roads were as necessary to travellers as the coaches and horses. Some were splendid places, where the traveller was met by a smiling landlord and a host of servants, grooms and waiters, ready with hot drinks and well-cooked dinners. Their beds had snow-white linen and were aired by copper warming-pans. Such inns were for wealthy travellers. They took in only the 'quality', gentry arriving in their own coaches or hired post-chaises. Others, which were far from comfortable, charged high prices for wretched food and dirty beds.

Inns which accommodated stage-coach passengers would not admit waggon company, unless they went into the kitchen and ate with the servants. But the servants of gentlefolk thought themselves far superior to the poor. Putting on airs and graces, they copied their masters and mistresses, and demanded a separate room for supper.

As for the poor foot-traveller, everyone looked down on him and often the door was slammed in his face. Servants shouted after him that a man who could not afford to travel in a better fashion might as well sleep under the hedge.

Waiters, chambermaids, grooms and postboys all expected a tip of sixpence or a shilling, and their rudeness was well known if the tip was not large enough. The coach-driver received sixpence from each passenger at the end of every stage.

The Golden Age of coaching

In the last thirty years of the Georgian period (1800–1830) traffic increased in speed and numbers beyond anything which had ever been known. Over 1000 vehicles left London every day, using altogether about 4000 horses. Fifteen kilometres on in all directions, and at stages all over the country, hundreds more horses were waiting to relieve them.

On Macadam's new roads travel by night became more common. The mail-coaches drove all day and night from every part of the kingdom, and arrived together at the Post Office in Lombard Street, London, at six o'clock in the morning.

Arguing about the bill

Mail-coaches departing from the General Post Office (above) and from the Gloucester Coffee House, Piccadilly, 1828

The stage-coaches ran faster and faster, and the sight of them, varnished and shining, their splendid horses driven by skilful coachmen, filled men with excitement and pleasure. Some men, indeed, spent much of their time riding in any new coach, on any fast run, for the sheer joy of it. The coachmen, if not quite so glorious as the mail-coach drivers, were lordly figures in their low-brimmed hats, striped waistcoats, topboots and huge driving coats, as they swaggered into the inn-yards, and took a glass of hot grog.

Their coaches all had names: *Magnet, Comet, Express, Lightning, Greyhound* and *Rocket,* and each had its rival belonging to another company, which would race neck and neck along Macadam's smooth roads. Speed was everything, and the drivers took a pride in arriving punctually at every stage.

As the coach drew near to its inn the guard sounded his horn. Fresh horses were brought out ready and were changed with all speed. There was time now only for a bite of food and a hasty pull at a mug of ale before the coach was off again.

The Oxford and 'Opposition' coaches racing each other

Traffic grew so great that at Hounslow near London, for instance, a famous coaching centre with many inns, 2500 horses were kept for posting. Large inns could stable as many as 600 horses.

On May-day each year the coaches and horses were decked with ribbons and flowers, and at Christmas with sprigs of holly, while the coachmen wore enormous buttonholes, and tied bows on their whips.

This, then, was the glorious age of coaching, the time when the coaches, the Royal Mail, the post-chaises, and all those oddly named vehicles already mentioned, drove down the road in a cloud of dust and splendour. But this glory came to a sudden end.

The railways arrived. In ten or fifteen years, by tremendously hard work, a network of railway lines spread all over the country. Train travel was cheaper, as one train could carry more passengers than 30 coaches. The coaches, the lordly inns and the host of drivers, grooms and servants were ruined.

A carrier's cart

A mail-coach starting at night

Shillibeer's horse omnibus, 1836

A sedan chair

Town travel in Georgian days

The most elegant form of travel for short journeys, in the eighteenth century, was by sedan chair. In days when rich and fashionable people wore silk clothes and astonishingly high hair styles, they needed some convenient form of transport through the narrow and muddy streets. They hired sedan chairs and were carried to the assembly or ball by two burly chairmen. The nobility had their own richly ornamented sedans, which stood in the lobby of their great homes, waiting until her ladyship was ready to go visiting.

Horse-drawn vehicles were used in town for many years, and in 1829 a man named Shillibeer started the first omnibus. It was drawn by three horses and ran from the City to a public-house on the Edgware Road called 'The Yorkshire Stingo'. As you can see, passengers were only carried inside.

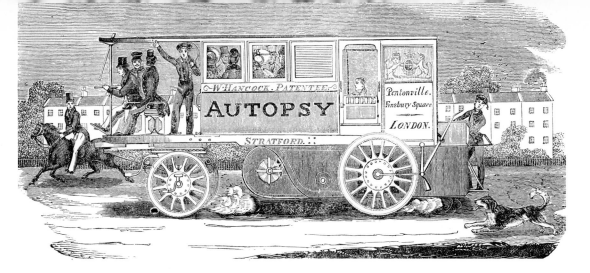

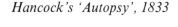

Hancock's 'Autopsy', 1833

From the 1820s, strange monsters appeared called steam-coaches. Trevithick, a Cornishman, pioneered the idea, but it was Dr Gurney who produced a steam-driven carriage in 1827 that carried 18 passengers at 16 km/h. He started a service from Bath, Walter Hancock ran one in London and Dr Church ran a fast service to Birmingham. Public alarm about accidents and enmity from railwaymen eventually forced these vehicles off the roads.

In 1810 the first bicycle, a French invention, appeared in England. It was known as the hobby horse, or dandy horse, and was built partly of wood and partly of iron. The rider swung his legs so that his toes touched the ground and pushed him along. The hobby horse soon went out of fashion, and fifty years passed before the boneshaker made its appearance.

Randolph's steam carriage, 1872

A hobby-horse

A midshipman

3 Ships and Sailors

During this period, Britain was building up her trade and increasing her Empire overseas. Her strength lay, not in the Army, but in the Royal Navy. Throughout the long wars with France many famous sea-battles, such as Quiberon Bay and the battle of Trafalgar, took place.

The press gang

In spite of the great importance of the Royal Navy, life on board His Majesty's ships was so hard that no man would willingly serve as an ordinary seaman unless he wished to escape from a crime or debt. The sailors' food was foul and often unfit to eat. They had no fresh vegetables, so scurvy was a common disease. Their sleeping quarters were cramped and unhealthy. Pay was scanty and often in arrears, yet discipline was iron-hard and brutal in the extreme.

When the sailors were needed for the Navy, they were usually obtained by force of the press gang. In seafaring towns, a party of sailors, led by an officer and all armed with cutlasses, would enter the taverns, shops and market to seize any likely-looking man and carry him off to serve as a seaman.

The press gang

The frigate 'Triton'

An admiral

A sailor

A cabin boy

Mariners and fishermen were taken from peaceful ships in harbour, merchant ships returning from voyages were often boarded on their way up Channel to London, husbands were snatched from their work and, it is said, a bridegroom and many of the congregation were once carried off from the church door!

Sailors in the Navy at this time had no official uniform, but the mark of a seaman was his thick short pigtail which stood out because it was stiffened with tar or grease.

Naval officers were no longer nobles from the Court, as in Charles II's time. Usually they were younger sons of gentlemen, who were sent to sea under the eye of a captain. They started with the rank of midshipman, and learned the art of seamanship the hard way.

Conditions in the Navy were so bad that there were serious mutinies during the French wars. Yet these ill-fed, ill-paid ruffians were the magnificent seamen who fought and died with Hawke and Nelson. There is little doubt that they were the finest sailors in the world.

A ship's cook

21

The 'Victory' at sea,
about 1780

The 'Royal George'

Ships

The *Royal George,* a ship of 2000 tons, is a fine example of an eighteenth-century ship. She was built at Woolwich in 1756 and was equipped with a hundred guns. She had the old-fashioned beaked bows and lanterns on her poop. She carried a bowsprit sail and a triangular lateen sail on the mizzen mast.

Nelson's flagship, the *Victory,* was of much the same size: 2162 tons and 57 metres long, and manned by a crew of 830 men. Her bows were not beaked, but were built as part of the hull. In Nelson's day she carried 102 guns, a mixture of 42-, 24- and 12-pounders which had a range of 400 to 600 yards. The guns blazed round shot and grape shot at the crowded decks of the ships they attacked, while sharp-shooters in the rigging picked off officers.

Sea-battles, such as Trafalgar, were fought at close quarters, and after several broadsides from the guns, boarding parties swarmed on to the enemy ships. When a ship was disabled or had lost so many of her crew that they could no longer work the ship, she hauled down her flag and surrendered.

Merchant ships were far more numerous than warships. There were West Indiamen, fast sloops of about 400 tons, which were known as 'slavers'. West Indiamen carried cotton goods from Liverpool to West Africa, exchanging them for slaves to take to the West Indies, and came home with cargoes of tobacco, sugar and rum. These fast ships were sometimes seized by mutinous crews and became pirate vessels, which, from their hideouts among the islands of the West Indies, preyed upon peaceful merchant shipping.

The great East Indiamen, engaged on trade with India and the Far East, were slower ships. They were well armed against pirates and against the French. They carried provisions for the long voyage round the Cape of Good Hope, lasting six months, and often were away from home for a year or more.

A West Indiaman

The first steamship

In 1802, after some years of experiment, a Scotsman named William Symington built a steam engine to drive a tugboat called the *Charlotte Dundas*. Her trials on a canal were most successful, but the canal-owners were afraid that the wash from her paddle-wheel would injure the canal banks, and she was never used again.

An East Indiaman

Thus Henry Bell's *Comet* of 1812 was the first steamship in regular service. She was a small ship with one 4 horse-power engine and a sail on her tall funnel. On her trips along the Scottish coast she reached the great speed of 12 km/h.

By 1821 steamers were making regular crossings between Dover and Calais, and men were talking of building iron ships. But these did not come for some time, and sailing ships still had a long and glorious age before them.

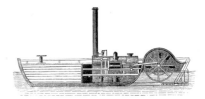

The 'Charlotte Dundas', 1802

The 'Comet', 1812

23

Smugglers

High taxes upon tea, silk and such French goods as wine, brandy and lace made smuggling a flourishing trade in the eighteenth century. People regarded smuggling as an almost innocent occupation, like poaching. The smugglers found it easy to supply the gentry with tea and brandy, and their ladies with lace, silk and gloves, on which not a penny in tax had been paid.

All along the coast, and especially in Kent and Sussex, smuggling was a regular trade, and the boatmen were helped by the local people. Goods were brought ashore at night from French boats or from homeward bound East Indiamen and were hidden in barns, cellars and even churches, until they could be safely taken to London. There were many desperate fights with the Customs Officers, for smugglers who were caught might be hanged or transported to a convict colony abroad.

A Revenue cutter chasing smugglers

How the sailors lived in a warship

The Bridgewater Canal

Canals

For a long time the rivers had carried considerable traffic, chiefly because the roads were so badly kept and waggons were slow. In the first half of the eighteenth century many rivers were deepened and widened, and locks were built so that barges could be raised or lowered to different water levels. In the middle of the eighteenth century came the great period of canal-making. The Duke of Bridgewater and his engineer James Brindley, built a canal from Worsley to Manchester, to carry coal from the Duke's mines. It was realised at once that here was a way of sending heavy goods from one place to another more quickly and cheaply than by slow-moving waggons on the roads.

Large gangs of labourers dug out the canal-beds and constructed bridges and aqueducts, which took the water-ways across the countryside. These labourers were called 'navvies', short for 'navigators', since the canals were built for 'inland navigation'.

The Manchester–Liverpool Canal was followed by the Grand Junction Canal, which joined the rivers Mersey and Trent, and soon a whole network of canals linking up the rivers spread all over England.

The Duke of Bridgewater

25

4 Houses in Georgian Days

The assembly room of a Georgian mansion

Chatsworth

Much of the wealth which came from increasing trade and from better farming methods was spent on building fine houses in both town and country. Perhaps the new houses did not have the warm friendliness of Tudor homes, but they were stately and noble. Many of them were designed in the style of Roman temples.

Great houses, such as Buckingham House and Blenheim Palace, were built with a splendid central block to which the kitchens on the one side and stables on the other were connected by a colonnade.

These great houses had magnificent assembly rooms which were richly decorated with statues, pillars and huge oil paintings in gilt frames. The ceilings and walls were covered with plaster designs and pictures, usually in the Italian style. The furnishings were lavish and elegant, and were often modelled on the new ideas brought home from abroad by the young lords.

A library designed by Adam

A town house

Robert Adam, a popular architect of this time, designed many of the lofty drawing-rooms in these great houses in his own style. Many of his rooms had curved ceilings, and plaster decorations in delicate shades of pink, green and blue. They were often rounded at one end.

Wooden panelling began to go out of fashion, and hand-painted wallpaper took its place. The fireplace of white marble had its coal fire in a raised, decorated grate, while above it was a gilt-framed mirror between silver candle-sticks. Elaborate glass chandeliers were used for lighting.

At its best, this style had noble dignity, and it suited the aristocrats, with their rich clothes, their powdered wigs and fine manners.

Small Georgian town houses

Georgian houses of moderate size were perhaps the most pleasant-looking houses ever built. Many of them are still to be seen in the older parts of English towns. The outside was usually plain and simple, of red brick or white stucco, with sash windows and a handsome doorway. Windows were carefully spaced, one pair exactly matching another, to give a feeling of balance to the house.

The roof was tiled and had dormer windows, but no gables. Attached to the wrought-iron railings in front of the house was a metal cone. Here the linkboy, after lighting her ladyship home at night, doused his flaming torch.

A particularly handsome doorway

The Circus at Bath

28

Inside these homes of well-to-do gentlefolk were comfortable rooms, lit by tall windows and furnished with carpets, rugs and graceful chairs. The furnishings were elegant, but they were not as extravagant as those in the great houses.

Chairs, sofas, side-tables and writing-desks were designed to suit the rooms and were arranged to stand in their exact places against the walls and in alcoves. Candles, for long the only means of lighting, began to be replaced by lamps which burned a fine whale-oil.

Town houses were often built, not separately, but in terraces and crescents, sometimes arranged as a 'square' with a garden in the middle. A Georgian terrace might contain 20 houses, all with identical doors, windows and balconies. Each house in the terrace was tall and narrow, perhaps one room wide, with kitchen, dining-room, drawing room and bedrooms rising one above another to the attics where the servants slept.

A room of about 1720

A town square at Bath

Gardens

The gardens and grounds of the great country houses were designed in a new style and were very different from the trim Tudor and Stuart gardens, with their clipped hedges, square flower beds and straight paths.

The fashionable idea was to bring the natural countryside right up to the big house and, at the same time, to provide a fine view down a wide avenue of trees. Immense sums of money were spent in laying out parks with artificial lakes and fountains, raised mounds, terraces and statues, pavilions and summer-houses, as well as clumps of trees and shrubs.

The experts in this 'landscape' gardening were William Kent and 'Capability' Brown, an odd character, who gained his name from his habit of always saying he saw 'capability of improvement' in an estate.

'Capability' Brown

A Chippendale settee and a Hepplewhite chair

Furniture

Georgian furniture became elegant and costly. The sturdy oak of earlier times gave place to more ornamental woods, such as walnut, beech and mahogany, and we begin to hear of chairs and tables being made in various styles, named after their makers.

A walnut chair, about 1720

The most famous names in furniture-making were Chippendale, Hepplewhite and Sheraton, who were three designers of furniture at this time. Examples of their work can still be seen today. Heppelwhite made his chairs, tables and sideboards more delicately than Chippendale, and for decoration he often used inlay patterns of different coloured woods. Sheraton made some beautiful furniture, but it was sometimes rather fussy and over-ornamented.

An English silver teapot

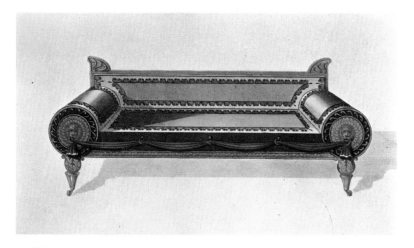

A Sheraton sofa

Trade with the East brought fresh ideas and new materials. Furniture was made of cane and bamboo, and Chinese patterns and designs were copied.

There was now more furniture in the houses than in Stuart times, and it was comfortably upholstered. Curtains, bed-hangings and cushions were made of wonderfully patterned materials, for rich people wanted their homes to be decorative as well as useful. There was a new interest in vases, statues and pottery, much of it in Greek and Roman styles. Pianos were invented by an Italian in 1709 and they gradually took the place of the spinet.

An upholstered chair

An early upright piano

An exotic bed designed by Sheraton

The People of Georgian Days 5

A fashionable couple, 1730

Their clothes

A Georgian gentleman wore a waisted coat, stiffened to make the skirts stand out. His wide cuffs were turned back to show the white shirt underneath and he wore a cravat at his throat. Wigs were usually tied behind, and for special occasions they were powdered and curled. When indoors, gentlemen wore a kind of turban or nightcap over their shaven heads. Three-cornered hats were popular, but they were no longer decorated with feathers. There was less lace worn than in Charles II's time and men's clothes were not of such bright colours. From this time onward they gradually became quieter and duller.

Men carried snuff boxes, since smoking was now considered a low habit, fit only for sailors and workmen.

Ladies' dresses were made of heavy, rich materials, and their skirts were either stretched over hoops or stiffened with whalebone. Their hair was worn in curls and ringlets, with a little lace cap, or a large straw hat on top. Every lady of fashion carried a fan with a jewelled handle.

Men's wigs

A turban

Ladies' wigs

By the end of the eighteenth century, ladies were wearing wigs and false hair, powdered and curled, and piled up into enormous shapes over small cushions. Imitation fruit, flowers and even ships were added as ornaments. A tax on powder put an end to this odd fashion.

Soon after the French Revolution, fashion changed dramatically. Heavy silks and rich brocades went out and were replaced by flimsy muslins and lawns, so that dresses became almost transparent. Ladies' waists moved up high, arms and shoulders were left bare or covered by light shawls. They now wore little slippers instead of high-heeled shoes.

'Empire line' dresses, about 1800 (left) and a dandy (right)

Men's coats became tight-waisted, with cutaway tails. Trousers became fashionable in place of knee-breeches, except for older gentlemen and on certain occasions at Court.

In London and down at Brighton, Beau Brummell, prince of the dandies, set the fashion for the 'bucks', as the smart young men were called. His dress included high turned-down collars, starched neckcloths, tight waists and very tight trousers fitting into riding-boots. Above all, clothes had to be perfectly cut and fitted.

Children's clothes

Children's clothes

Until Georgian times, children were dressed exactly like their parents, but now they began to have their own styles. The fashion for girls to wear long drawers down to their ankles, called pantaloons, lasted for many years.

Soldiers

The Army became more popular during Wellington's struggle with the French. Laurel-decked coaches often carried the news of his victories to town and village. The ordinary soldiers in the Army were the lowest, roughest men in the land, for only crime, drink or unemployment would make a man join the ranks. Wellington called them 'the scum of the earth', though he added they made 'fine fellows' in the end. The discipline of the sergeants was very hard, and punishment was usually the lash. Yet in battle, these men repeatedly proved themselves tough, brave, disciplined soldiers.

An Infantryman, 1742

A Lancer

35

The officers were sons of lords and rich men who bought their places for large sums of money, and looked on soldiering as an expensive hobby. Even in the long war against Napoleon, they continued to dress like dandies, to attend balls and to go hunting. Wellington found some of them putting up umbrellas in battle to protect their fine uniforms!

The uniforms of this period were brightly coloured: red coats, white breeches and black boots. In time, the full-skirted coat with wide cuffs changed to a cut-away jacket. Hats and caps varied according to regiments.

Ordinary soldiers were paid only two or three shillings a week, but prices were low. They could get drunk for a very few pence. Their lives were rough and hard, but they had to keep their uniforms in good order.

Weapons

Swords, cutlasses and daggers went out of fashion in the Army, except for officers and cavalry. The ordinary soldier relied on his musket and bayonet. His musket was a heavy gun weighing 7 kg, and must have been tiring to carry on long marches. Soldiers marched everywhere and often went into action after a night march of 10 or 20 kilometres. Gunpowder charges were carried in paper packets, called cartridges, but the flint, which lasted for about 20 shots, was useless in rain.

A musket was accurate up to 50 or 100 metres, so the troops fought in two ranks, the front rank kneeling down. When all fired together, it was called a volley. British troops were famous for holding their fire until the enemy was very near. They then fired a volley and followed it up with a bayonet charge. After a halt, they reformed their ranks, and reloaded.

The cannons, or artillery, were mounted on wheels or gun carriages and pulled by horses. They fired round-shot, cannon balls and shrapnel a distance of about one kilometre.

A Grenadier, 1742

A Trooper of the 23rd Dragoons, 1809

Cannon at the Battle of Waterloo

The people's work 6

Enclosures

All through Georgian times, tremendous changes were taking place in the country districts. For centuries, much of the land had been farmed in open fields, divided into strips, which the farmers and peasants rented from the Lord of the Manor. The poor countryman eked out his living by keeping a few animals, geese, ducks or chickens on the common-land, and also by spinning and weaving in his cottage.

The big landowners now wanted to get rid of this strip-farming so that larger farms could be made and more efficient methods of farming used. Parliament passed the Enclosure Acts which enabled owners to divide the land into compact farms. Peasants, faced with fencing costs, often sold their few strips cheaply as they generally lost their grazing rights on the common-land.

Hedges were planted and the land was divided into fields. Sometimes several fields were let out as farms to farmers with money of their own, but they were charged a higher rent than before. The owner farmed the rest of the land himself. Gradually the common-land was enclosed too, the woods were cut down and neat plantations of trees took their place.

There was a tradition for milkmaids and sweeps to dance together on May Day

The village green

Threshing swedes

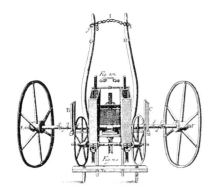

A cultivator

These new farms grew larger quantities of corn than the strips had done. Prices were high owing to the wars with France, and the landowners and farmers made their fortunes.

New methods of farming

Instead of leaving fields to lie fallow for a year, Lord Townshend (often known as 'Turnip' Townshend), began growing turnips, to be used in winter for cattle and sheep fodder. Better grass was grown for hay, and it was no longer necessary to kill off nearly all the cattle in autumn, and to salt down their flesh. Fresh meat could now be bought in winter, which meant that the disease called scurvy became less common and the people's health improved.

Thomas Coke, who lived at Holkham in Norfolk, improved his land by careful farming, and produced a fine breed of sheep. People came from all over England and Europe to see his fine animals, and to watch the Holkham sheep-shearings.

Jethro Tull's wheat drill

Thomas Coke of Norfolk

38

Robert Bakewell of Leicestershire greatly improved the quality of his farm animals, and other farmers followed his example. The animals at Smithfield Meat Market doubled in weight during the eighteenth century.

Jethro Tull, in Queen Anne's reign, had invented a machine which sowed corn in neat rows. The seed was spread evenly and the land could be weeded and hoed between the rows of young shoots. This new method of sowing, which took the place of scattering by hand, together with new ideas about manuring, produced heavier crops. Tull also invented a simple threshing machine; a number of sticks were set in motion, and they beat out the corn from the ear.

A mantrap; the spikes gripped a poacher's leg. The usual penalty for poaching was transportation

Poor countryfolk

Poor countryfolk found that the few guineas paid to them for their land did not last very long. Some managed to buy another small piece of land, but even so, life was difficult for them. They had lost the common-land, where they had kept a cow, a pig or two and some geese. The woods, which had given them firewood and an occasional hare or rabbit, were cut down or guarded by gamekeepers with guns and steel traps.

Another change was taking place. With the coming of machines and factories, spinning and weaving in the cottages was dying out. The peasants, distressed and angry, went off to the towns to look for work in the new factories. Often there was no work for men, but only for women and children who were paid a lower wage than a man.

If he was fortunate, a peasant might find work on a farm as a labourer for a shilling a day. This was not enough to feed his family upon, so his wife worked in the fields also. When the price of bread rose very high, he was given a little money from the poor rates.

Scottish crofter women still used a distaff for spinning

Cotton factory, Union Street, Manchester

Countrymen were tempted to work in the new factories

Work in the towns

In the days of the Stuarts and in the times of George I and George II, nearly everything that ordinary people needed, clothes, tools, bread, meat and beer, was made in their own villages. Only the wealthy sent to London for books, furniture, china and such fine things.

By the end of the Georgian age, new 'manufacturing' towns had sprung up near the coalmines and iron industry, mostly in the Midlands and North of England. People now worked together in large numbers, in factories, instead of at home with their families.

Inventors

Spinning is the process of making raw wool or cotton, after it has been carded, into a thread. This was done for hundreds of years by hand-spinning, and later with a spinning wheel.

Weaving is the process of making the spun thread into cloth, by passing a shuttle in and out between cross threads, like darning. For many years this had been done on a machine worked by one weaver, who threw the shuttle from one hand to the other.

40

Dressing cloth in Yorkshire (left) and two factory children (right)

In 1733 John Kay invented a Flying Shuttle which made weaving so quick that faster spinning was needed to keep up with the weavers. By 1764 James Hargreaves, himself a poor weaver, through watching his wife Jenny at her wheel, was able to perfect a spinning machine which kept pace with the weavers. He called it his Spinning Jenny.

Next, Richard Arkwright, a barber, who listened to talk about machines while on his way round the mills selling wigs, made a spinning machine, worked not by hand but by water-power. Samuel Crompton made an even better machine called a Mule, and spinning went ahead of weaving.

Later came steam-power, which really caused factories to take the place of cottage work. James Watt's name is always linked with early steam-engines, but he was not their inventor. He was an instrument-maker in Glasgow, who one day was asked to repair an early steam-engine. A man called Newcomen is said to have made the first steam-engine. Watt saw its faults and began to work on a better model. He found a partner in Matthew Boulton of Birmingham, and together they set up a factory there. By 1781 they had made a steam-engine which could drive machinery.

The Spinning Jenny

Brutal overseers in charge of child factory workers

A clergyman, the Reverend Edmund Cartwright, now invented a weaving loom driven by one of these steam-engines. This new way of driving machines was quickly used for flour, silk, cotton and saw-mills.

Factories were built and fitted with these new machines, and thread and cloth were produced more quickly and cheaply than by the old methods. Unemployed folk from the country came to work in the factories, and rows of cheap, shoddily built houses were put up for them, as near to the factories as possible. No thought was given to fresh air, water supply, beauty or cleanliness, and they soon became slums.

As the population was growing, there were plenty of workers wanting jobs, so wages were low and hours of work very long. Men could not earn enough, so their little children at the age of six or seven years went to work all day in the factories with them. If they grew tired they were beaten awake by the 'strapper'; if they went to sleep they often fell into the machinery and were injured or killed.

Cloth was produced very cheaply at this time, and as trade increased, the mill-owners became very rich, but most of the workers remained poor and miserable. Only a very few were able to save enough money to start factories of their own.

Of course, it must not be thought that all the working people of England were suddenly forced into factories and slums. Most of the skilled trades continued to flourish in the small workshops of the towns and villages: the clockmakers, tailors, blacksmiths, harness-makers, carpenters and coach-builders were craftsmen who could do their work far better than machines. The hosts of servants in big houses and inns, the ostlers, grooms and all those engaged in the coaching business, the farm-workers and the fisherfolk had never heard of the dark, gloomy factories in the north of England.

The blacksmith's job was just as it had always been

A milkwoman and a lamplighter

7 The People at Play in Georgian England

Swordfights between fencing masters were given before large crowds, who were disappointed if one of the fencers was not seriously wounded

The sports and pastimes of Stuart England were cruel and bloodthirsty, and although the Georgian Age was less savage, many of the same sports were carried on, for people do not change their ways suddenly. There were still the old Bankside sports of bull and bear baiting, sword-fights and cock-fighting. An advertisement of this time says:

> A mad bull to be dressed up with fireworks and turned loose. A dog to be dressed up with fireworks all over and turned loose with the bull. Also a bear to be turned loose and a cat to be tied to the bull's tail.

This was the age of duels. To settle a dispute, gentlemen would 'call each other out' to fight with swords or pistols. A wound usually ended the duel, but men were sometimes killed.

A duel

Prize-fighting, with bare knuckles, was the forerunner of modern boxing. Fights were held in the open air and lasted 50, 60 or even 100 rounds. Prize-fights were forbidden by law, but as they were so popular with the gentlemen of fashion, who gambled on the fight, they took place regularly in fields and commons just outside London. When the news went round that a contest was to be held, all the roads leading to the spot were thronged with every kind of cart, chaise, coach and carriage, jostling their way to the match.

Cock-fighting, horse-racing and even donkey-racing for the chimney-sweeps, were excuses for gambling; people also took bets on such odd contests as pudding- or tripe-eating matches!

Cricket now became a popular team game, with recognised rules. As early as 1744 Kent played All-England and beat them by 111 notches to 110. The score was kept by cutting a notch on a stick for each run. Below you can see the early wicket and club-like bat. By 1830 three stumps and a broad bat were in use, and round-arm bowling was taking the place of underarm bowling.

A prizefight—Broome v. Hannan near Bicester in Oxfordshire, 1841, for a prize of £1000

Cricket in 1743; notice the wicket keeper who has removed his wig, and the scorer who cuts a notch for each run

45

Lady Fair at Southwark, drawn by Hogarth

Fairs

The great London fair, St Bartholomew's at Smithfield, was still held every year, with its stalls, sideshows, wrestling and merry-go-rounds. It became so rowdy and lawless that the authorities finally closed it down in 1855.

There were several other fairs, including Lady Fair at Southwark, which is shown above in Hogarth's amusing picture. On the left, a stage is collapsing on to an ale booth, though the actress with the drum continues to advertise the show. There is another show just starting at the back, a flying man, a peep-show in the foreground and a fencing master on horseback.

Hunting

The games and amusements mentioned so far were those which everyone could enjoy, but there were other amusements for the 'gentry', the large number of aristocrats and well-to-do folk who had plenty of money from their estates or factories. Hunting was their favourite outdoor sport. Deer hunts were now rare, but fox-hunting, with all the added excitement and skill of jumping hedges, took their place. The older sport of hunting the hare was even more popular, since a hare does not run so far afield as a fox.

Fox-hunting

46

The London Season

One of the chief events of the year was the London 'Season', when the country gentry came up to spend a few weeks in London. They hired houses in a fashionable part of the town and brought their sons, daughters and servants with them. They came to see the sights and to enter the fashionable world at the assemblies, dances and balls which were given every night.

Other places had their 'season' also. The most famous were Tunbridge Wells and Bath, to which the gentry went to drink the waters for their health, and also to enjoy the company, the balls and the gambling for high stakes.

Vauxhall Gardens; balloon ascents from the gardens were very popular

The Pump Room at Bath

At Bath the gaming table was a centre of attraction. Hazard and faro were played, and, in later years, whist. Large fortunes and estates were sometimes gambled away in a night

Bath

Bath was the most fashionable town in England. The baths made by the Romans were still in use, and these became popular in Stuart and Georgian times. In the eighteenth century, the town was rebuilt in the new elegant style, and it remains today a wonderful example of Georgian building.

Drinking in the magnificent Pump Room gradually became more popular than bathing. But the beauties and the dandies came not only to drink the waters; they came to dance at the balls, to show off their clothes and to be taught the perfection of elegant behaviour by the lord and master of Bath—Beau Nash, the best-dressed man in England.

Seaside resorts

Although the British are a seafaring people, no one had thought of bathing in the sea until this time. In fact, people rarely even visited the seaside until Georgian days, when it suddenly became fashionable to visit the new seaside resorts of Brighton, Weymouth, Scarborough and Margate. People bathed from curious little bathing huts on wheels, which were pulled by horses to the water. When he was Prince Regent, George IV was very fond of Brighton. He spent much time there, and built an elaborate house in the style of an Eastern Palace which is known as the Pavilion.

Coffee-houses

Coffee-houses were still popular with citizens, merchants, writers, lawyers and clergymen. They all had their favourite house at which they called every morning to chat, to drink and to hear the latest news. For a penny they could borrow a newspaper.

At one time there were three thousand of these coffee-houses in London. Doctor Johnson, the writer and maker of the famous Dictionary, was well known for his conversation, and men crowded round him in the coffee-houses to listen to his talk on every subject. The nobility now began to meet at clubs instead of at the coffee-houses.

Dr Johnson

A coffee house early in the eighteenth century

'The Times' newspaper of 7 November 1805— with the news of the Battle of Trafalgar

Newspapers

For a long time there had been newsletters such as *The Spectator* and *The Tatler*, which gave the happenings of the day. News could also be heard in the coffee-houses, and at one of them Edward Lloyd became famous for his daily news about ships.

By George III's reign, printed newspapers appeared regularly at twopence and threepence each. They had four pages and included news about Parliament, letters, poetry and advertisements.

Lloyd's Coffee House was the centre for shipping news

The oldest English newspaper, Berrow's *Worcester Journal* appeared in 1690. *The Daily Courant* (1702) was the first daily, and the *Evening Post* (1705) the first evening paper. Other early papers were the *Morning Post* and *The Times* (1785), but their price was too high for the ordinary citizen, so many people would share a paper between them.

The Streets in Georgian Days 8

'Pots to mend!'

'Lily white vinegar, threepence a quart!'

The streets were roughly paved and without kerbstones, and posts protected the pathway, on which the chairmen were forbidden to carry their sedan chairs. Foul water and refuse ran down the middle of the road in a gutter. Signboards hung outside every house, announcing who lived there. Bow-windows, steps and porches jutted out into the path.

The noise of the street-criers, the bawling of the apprentices and shop-keepers, 'Rally, ladies, rally! Buy! Buy! Buy!', the rumble of heavy carts and coaches, the shouts and quarrelling of the waggoners made a terrific din in the streets, to which was added the confusion caused by droves of animals going to be slaughtered.

Bands of young nobles who called themselves 'Mohocks' made the streets dangerous at night by their rowdy behaviour. They insulted passers-by, tipped over sedan chairs, tripped up the Watch and assaulted the 'Charlies'.

'Sixpence a pound, fair cherries!'

A fishmonger's stall

'Buy a fork or a fire shovel?'

The new gas lights in Pall Mall, 1809

Besides the respectable tradesmen, workers and street sellers, there were hordes of poor and destitute who seldom had regular work, but lived as best they could. Thieving, robbery and murder were common crimes and punishments were savage. A man could be hanged for any one of two hundred crimes, such as sheep-stealing, pocket-picking, or, indeed, for the theft of above five shillings.

A public hanging was an entertainment which attracted huge crowds, who accompanied the condemned wretch through the streets with cheers and songs, or waited all night, enjoying themselves, outside Newgate Prison.

Street lighting, with oil lamps, made the way safer at night, while gas lamps, which appeared in 1807, excited great astonishment.

A hawker of old clothes

An Irish watchman, 5 November 1829. He shouted: 'Therefore take care of fire and candlelight, 'Tis a fine Thursday morning and so goodnight.'

Peelers in 1851

Quelling a riot. Soldiers were sometimes called in

The police

There was much crime in these days, for the old watchmen were feeble and frightened, and the chances of arrest were small. In 1780 the mob burned down 70 houses and 4 prisons. There were no police to stop them and the soldiers had to be called out.

The forerunners of our modern police were the Bow Street Runners. They were started by Henry Fielding, a magistrate at the Bow Street court. The Bow Street Runners wore red waistcoats and were often called Robin Redbreasts. They were a detective force rather than policemen, for their jobs were to raid gambling houses, to pursue robbers and highwaymen and to track down murderers and wanted criminals. Unlike the British police today, they were armed with pistols.

In 1829 the place of the Bow Street Runners was taken by the Metropolitan Police. Under Sir Robert Peel a body of 3000 men was recruited to bring law and order to London. Every part of London was patrolled by a policeman in uniform.

The first policemen wore top hats, blue coats, leather belts and white trousers, and each carried a truncheon and a rattle, which was used to call for extra help. At first, the 'Bobbies' or 'Peelers' as they were called, were regarded with suspicion and they were jeered at, but sensible citizens soon realised the value of their work. The streets became safer than ever before.

A Bow Street runner

9 Some Important Events in Queen Victoria's Reign

Queen Victoria at the time of her Coronation

Victoria reigned from 1837 to 1901. She married her cousin, Prince Albert, in 1840. The chief ministers of her long reign were Peel, Palmerston, Salisbury, Gladstone and Disraeli.

1840 Sir Rowland Hill started the Penny Post. Railways were being built all over Britain. Hunger and poverty was widespread, but trade was increasing.

1851 Prince Albert organised The Great Exhibition, housed in the Crystal Palace in Hyde Park. British goods were shown to visitors from all over the world.

1854–1856 The Crimean War was fought by Britain and France against Russia. Florence Nightingale, by nursing the wounded, began her life's work for hospitals.

1857 The Indian Mutiny.

1865 Lister, a famous surgeon, was using antiseptics.

1869 Opening of the Suez Canal.

1870 The Education Act introduced Board (or state) schools.

1850–1900 Until Victoria's reign, little was known in Europe about the interior of Africa, but the discoveries of Speke and Burton, and the explorations of David Livingstone and an American journalist H M Stanley, opened up the 'Dark Continent'. Cecil Rhodes founded Rhodesia and added vast lands to the British Empire.

The Great Exhibition of 1851 at the Crystal Palace

1899–1902 The South African War was fought between the Dutch settlers (Boers) and the British. Lord Kitchener and Baden-Powell, who later founded the Boy Scouts, made their names in this war.

A new invention—the steam plough

Throughout this reign there were a great many inventions and engineering triumphs. The chief of these were:

1838 Two steamships crossed the Atlantic in nineteen days. The first telegraph service in England was set up by Wheatstone and Cooke.
1858 The first trans-Atlantic cable was laid.
1862 The first London trams (horse-drawn).
1863 London's Underground Railway was opened.
1869 The 'boneshaker' bicycle appeared.
1876 Bell's first telephone (in Boston, USA).
1878 First public telephone exchange in London.
1880 First cargoes of frozen meat from abroad.
1884 Daimler's motor-car engine.
1885 Benz made the first motor-car (in Germany). Stanley's Safety Bicycle.
1888 Dunlop's air-filled tyres.
1897 Marconi and Oliver Lodge experimenting with wireless in London.
1901 Marconi received the first trans-Atlantic wireless signal.

A gramophone of 1900; the record was a wax cylinder

There were many famous writers in Victoria's reign, of whom Charles Dickens was the most popular.

1837 *Pickwick Papers* **1848** *David Copperfield*

Of the children's books, two of the most famous were:

1866 *Alice in Wonderland* **1883** *Treasure Island*

A sewing machine, 1865

10 The Coming of the Railways

The arrival of the railways brought the Golden Age of coaching to a sudden end. For a number of years trucks had been used in the coalmining districts of the North of England and South Wales. They ran on wooden rails and carried coal down to the canals and rivers, and to the coal-ships bound for London. By 1810 iron rails were in use, because they did not wear out so quickly as wooden ones.

A Newcastle chaldron, carrying coal on wooden rails

Steam-engines

The first steam-engine which really worked was built by Thomas Newcomen in 1712 and was used to pump water out of a Cornish tin-mine. James Watt greatly improved this model, so that steam power could be used to drive machinery in factories and mills.

Such steam-engines were fixtures, and no self-moving engine had been invented until Nicholas Cugnot, a young Frenchman, built a curious monster called a steam carriage. Great crowds gathered to see him drive it in the streets of Paris. Cugnot's machine overturned when rounding a corner, and this so alarmed the French authorities that Cugnot and his machine were locked up.

Cugnot's steam car of 1769 ran out of control and demolished a wall

Trevithick's steam railway engine on display in London, on the site of the present Euston Station

As far as we know, William Murdoch, an engineer in the firm of Boulton & Watt, made the first self-moving engine in England. It is said that he made a small model and, after trying it out in his room, took it at dusk into a quiet lane, where its sparks and snorting so frightened a passing clergyman that he thought it was the devil!

For some reason, Murdoch gave up his experiments, but he told their secrets to young Richard Trevithick, who made a model engine so successfully that he took it to London and put it in a show.

Then Trevithick built the world's first railway engine, which pulled ten tons of iron along one of the early rail tracks in South Wales. Two difficulties arose: the rails kept breaking and the workers refused to let his engine run, because they were afraid that the men who looked after the horses would soon be out of work. Discouraged, Trevithick went off to South America to try to make his fortune.

The next engine was built at Leeds and was called *Blenkinsop's Rack Locomotive,* because it had a gear wheel which fitted into the teeth of a rack laid alongside the rails. But this idea did not last in England and, in 1813, Hedley's *Puffing Billy* and its sister *Wylam Dilly* were built without this device. They ran successfully up and down the line at Wylam Colliery, near Newcastle, pulling trucks of coal.

Blenkinsop's rack locomotive of 1812 (below, left) and 'Puffing Billy', 1813 (below, right)

Trains on the Liverpool and Manchester Railway

Opening of the Stockton and Darlington Railway, 27 September 1825

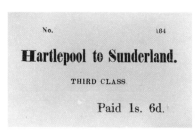

An early railway ticket

The first public railway

It was at Wylam that George Stephenson was born. He was the son of a poor man and he did not go to school. He had to wait until he was eighteen before he could pay for lessons in reading and writing. Stephenson became an engineer, and when he heard about *Puffing Billy* he went over to Wylam, his old home, to see it for himself. Presently, he persuaded his employer, the owner of the coalmine where he worked, to let him build a locomotive. He constructed one similar to *Puffing Billy* and called it *Blucher,* after the Prussian general who was at Waterloo with Wellington.

Stephenson now began his great work of building locomotives. Parliament, after a great deal of argument, gave permission for him to build a railway line between Stockton and Darlington. This line, the first public railway line, was opened in 1825. Its first train, pulled by Stephenson's engine called *Locomotion,* travelling at the great speed of 19 km/h, was made up of 12 trucks of coal and 21 waggons filled with passengers.

The Rainhill Trials

After this triumph came the famous Rainhill Trials. A railway line from Manchester to Liverpool was planned, and Stephenson was put in charge of the difficult task of laying the line, part of which ran over swampy land. It took him three years to finish the track, and then the owners were uncertain whether the waggons should be pulled along by horses, by cable or by locomotives. Eventually they offered a prize of £500 for the best engine. The trials were held at Rainhill in 1829, and the engines made 10 trips up and down a stretch of line 3 km long. Four engines entered the competition: the *Novelty,* the *Perseverance,* the *Sans Pareil*

and the *Rocket*, which was built by George Stephenson and his son Robert. Reaching a speed of 47 km/h, the *Rocket* easily won the prize and brought fame to the Stephensons.

The railway craze

After the Rainhill Trials nothing could stop the spread of railways. People tumbled over each other in their eagerness to subscribe money towards the opening of new railway lines to Birmingham, to Bristol, to Leeds and to every town of any size and importance. These lines were rapidly built by gangs of labourers or navvies.

There were, of course, people who had objected to the railways. Some land-owners refused to allow the lines to run through their estates, which is one of the reasons why certain towns today have their railway stations some distance away. But despite many difficulties, the railways spread rapidly, and only fifteen years after the *Rocket's* triumph, people were travelling in trains all over the country. The stage-coach companies were ruined, and the last run of the mail-coach was drawing near.

The rule book of the North Midlands Railway, 1840

The 'Rocket'

Building a railway; every cutting and embankment was dug by hand

59

Travelling on the new railways

Travel by the old stage-coaches had never been very comfortable, especially for the outside passengers, and the new railway carriages were no great improvement. First-class carriages had cushioned seats, but the roofs were low and the windows small, so that they were stuffy in summer and cold in winter, since no heating was provided.

The second-class carriages had wooden benches, and the third class carriages had no seats and no roof. They were just open trucks, and it is easy to imagine how miserable a journey could be on a wet, cold day.

Up to date luggage in 1884

Euston Station

Travelling First Class and travelling Third Class

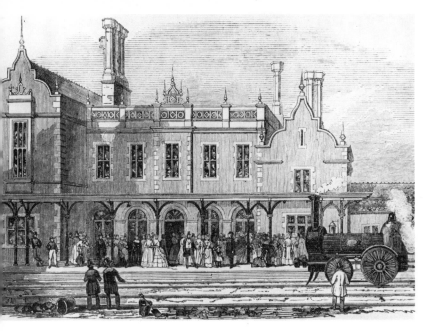

Tamworth Station

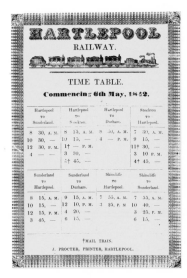

Timetable for a new railway service

Although travel by rail was uncomfortable, the journey was far quicker and cheaper than by stage-coach. This was partly because Parliament insisted that the railways must carry third-class passengers at a penny a mile. Ordinary people could travel to places which their fathers had never seen.

At first there were no signal-boxes. The driver simply kept a look-out for anything on the line and the passengers hoped his brakes were good. The first signalmen, called railway policemen, used flags and lamps, while signals were round or square boards on poles.

Gauges

Stephenson laid his rails with a width, or gauge, of 4 ft 8½ inches, which is now the standard gauge of most railways. As more and more railways were built, it became clear that their rails should be the same distance apart, or it would be impossible for rolling-stock to pass from one line to another.

The famous engineer, Brunel, chose a gauge of seven feet for the Great Western Railway, which he claimed would give smoother running and greater speeds. This gauge proved a nuisance, and in the end, the Great Western had to change to Stephenson's standard gauge of 4 ft 8½ inches.

An early signal

61

A workmen's train on the London Underground, 1872

The first underground railway

Thousands of passengers came to London by train and added their numbers to the streets, already overcrowded with horse-omnibuses, hansom cabs, carriages and waggons. Some people suggested that the traffic problem would be helped by building overhead or underground railways. Finally, despite many jokes about such an idea, it was decided to run trains in tunnels under the ground.

The Metropolitan Railway, opened in 1863, was the first of its kind. It was not very far below ground because chimneys and vents had to be made to let out the smoke from steam engines. By 1890 engineers had discovered how to run trains driven by electric motors, and gradually the London Underground grew to its present size. It is now the largest underground railway in the world.

The first electric underground trains at Stockwell Station

62

Town Traffic 11

A steam coach

Steam-coaches

In the towns the horse remained as important as ever for more than half a century. Steam-coaches in the streets had started to carry passengers as early as the railways, but in 1862 Parliament made a law that a horseless carriage must not travel faster than two miles per hour in the town, and a man with a red flag must walk sixty yards ahead of it. With this law steam-coaches disappeared from the roads, and town traffic was again horse-drawn.

A hansom cab

The hansom cab

Sedan chairs had almost vanished from the London streets before Victoria came to the throne, and soon the heavy hackney-coaches were ousted by the hansom cab, named after its inventor Joseph Hansom. Its neat appearance, with the cabby up behind, made it one of the everyday sights of London throughout Victoria's reign and until well into the twentieth century.

One of the last 'growler' cabs

Horse-drawn buses

The Victorian horse-omnibuses were painted red, green, blue, chocolate, yellow and white, according to their route, so that passengers looked for the colour of their bus, not for its number.

To get as many passengers as possible, the drivers of the rival omnibus companies raced at top speed between bus stops, where the conductors leapt down and snatched passers-by on board, or fought their rivals for the waiting passengers!

The early horse-bus carried its passengers inside, and there were a couple of seats on the box, next to the driver. So many people came to London for the Great Exhibition of 1851 that the omnibus companies took the daring step of putting passengers on the roof. Those who travelled on the roof sat back-to-back on long forms. Only men went 'on top' since ladies in their long, trailing skirts could not be expected to climb the iron ladder.

A horse omnibus, about 1830

A London double-decker horse bus

A famous painting showing the inside of a horse bus

The 'ordinary'

A racing cyclist

Cycling on a country road

Bicycles

In 1868, over fifty years after the *dandy-horse*, came the *boneshaker*, with its wooden wheels and iron tyres. It had pedals and so was the forerunner of the modern bicycle. There was no chain, and the pedals were fixed to the front wheel. When going downhill the pedals whizzed round so fast that the rider had to take his feet off them.

Next came the *ordinary*, usually known as the *penny-farthing*, with its huge front wheel and at the back a little one, only about 36 cm across. The pedals were fixed to the front hub, so by one turn of the pedals, the big wheel carried the rider forward a considerable distance.

He sat perched up 1·5 metres in the air, and pedalled furiously along the roads in a cloud of dust. Riding a penny-farthing was hard and even dangerous work. It was not long before steel, instead of wood, was used for bicycles, and solid rubber tyres were fitted. Even so, only the most daring of ladies would mount a bicycle. Tricycles were considered much safer.

A boneshaker

65

A safety bicycle and a delivery tricycle in 1892

Riding an ordinary

An advertisement of 1885 for an early safety bicycle

The first bicycle to resemble those that we ride nowadays was *Mr Starley's safety bicycle,* a Rover, made at Coventry in 1885. The wheels were of equal size, and its pedals drove it along by means of a chain connected to the back hub. Three years later came Dunlop's pneumatic or air-filled tyres, which made riding much more comfortable.

With the arrival of the safety bicycle many ladies took up cycling. It would have been impossible, however to cycle in the long, flowing skirts which were fashionable, so a special cycling outfit was invented, called the Rational Costume. Lady cyclists wore a man's Norfolk jacket, a trilby hat, woollen stockings and knickerbockers.

The steamship

While Trevithick, Hedley and Stephenson were using steampower to drive locomotives, other engineers were trying to use this same power in ships. As already mentioned on page 23, Symington's *Charlotte Dundas* and Bell's little *Comet* were in use before Waterloo. By 1815 steamers appeared on the river Thames and were making cross-Channel trips.

In 1825 the General Steam Navigation Company, the oldest ocean-going steamship company in the world, had 15 steamers, some of only 240 tons with two 40 hp engines, engaged on trade between London and the ports of Europe.

The little wooden *Savannah* of 300 tons was the first steamship to cross the Atlantic (1818). During the next twenty years, regular crossings were made, and were much faster than voyages by sailing ship. The paddle-steamers *Sirius* and *Great Western* made the crossing in 19 days (1838), while sailing ships usually took about 33 days.

A steam vessel about 1817

The 'William Fawcett', one of the first ships of the P & O Line

The Caledonia in 1842

Isambard Kingdom Brunel at the launching of the Great Eastern during 1857

The P & O Line (Peninsular and Orient) started with the little *William Fawcett,* which sailed from Falmouth to Gibraltar in 1837, and soon, other P & O ships were making trips to India and the East.

Three years later, Samuel Cunard founded the famous Cunard Line, which for many years rivalled the White Star Company on the Atlantic. His ship *Britannia,* a vessel of over 1000 tons, had engines of 740 hp and sailed at ten knots. (A knot is a speed of one sea mile an hour, 1·85 km or 1·15 miles.) She crossed the Atlantic in 14 days.

People scoffed at the idea of building ships of iron instead of oak until an iron ship, the *Great Britain,* built to the plans of I K Brunel, crossed the Atlantic in 15 days. About a year later she went aground on the Irish coast, but she was saved, because she was made of iron. A wooden ship would have been broken up by the waves. The arrival of iron ships meant that larger vessels could be built, though no one dreamed of liners so vast as the *Queen Elizabeth II.*

Here we must mention the *Great Eastern,* for she was the wonder and the failure of her age. When Brunel designed this ship, the biggest ship in the world was about 3400 tons. He planned to make the *Great Eastern* 18 000 tons.

This vast ship was designed to carry 4000 passengers and a large cargo, as well as the coal needed to drive the engines. For long voyages, sailing ships were still at an advantage, since they did not have to carry coal. All available space was used for cargo. The *Great Eastern* had paddles, and also a screw, but this idea did not work, because a screw could not function properly in water churned up by paddles. She had five funnels and six masts, and she was so big that she had to be launched sideways into the Thames at Millwall. Unfortunately she stuck fast for several months and her owners went bankrupt.

She was sold and put on the Atlantic crossing instead of the long Australian route for which she was designed. Her speed was 14 knots, but her great size could not be fully used in those days, and she did not pay her running costs.

The Great Eastern at sea

In 1865–66 the *Great Eastern* helped to lay the telegraph cables across the Atlantic, but after that useful job was finished, she was just a curiosity. For a time she was used as a floating fair, but finally she was broken up for scrap iron.

Despite the failure of the *Great Eastern*, the steamship had come to stay, but there was still a glorious spell of life ahead for sailing-ships. On very long voyages, such as those from India, China and Australia, round the Cape of Good Hope, the sailing ships were not only more useful, but actually faster, especially for such cargoes as tea and wool, which needed to reach their markets quickly.

The clippers

The clipper ships, sometimes called windjammers, were specially built for fast sailing to China and Australia. The Americans led the way at first with better ships, but British firms began to build equally well. Many a famous race took place when tea and wool clippers beat up the Channel, carrying every possible yard of canvas, in the effort to win the prize offered by merchants for the first ship to dock at London.

The Cutty Sark in dry dock at Greenwich

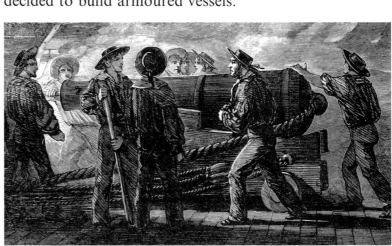

The clippers Ariel and Taeping in a famous race to dock in London with the first tea of the season

The clippers were wonderful ships and masterpieces of craftsmanship. They were faster than almost any steamer afloat, being capable of 17 knots. Of all these graceful ships, perhaps the most famous was the *Cutty Sark,* built as a tea-clipper and afterwards used on the Australian wool run.

Eventually steamships defeated the clippers, for the opening of the Suez Canal provided a shorter route to the East. This route was useless to sailing ships, as they would be becalmed on the canal for lack of wind. By 1890 the day of the clippers was almost over and only a few continued to make the long trip from Australia.

The Navy

Throughout Victoria's reign, the Royal Navy changed slowly from sail to steam, from wood to iron to steel— slowly because Nelson's victories had made Britain supreme at sea and there seemed no reason for rapid change. However, when the Navy's wooden ships came under fire from Russian forts during the Crimean war of 1854, it was decided to build armoured vessels.

Officers' wardroom on HMS Collingwood, 1845

Lashing hammocks on HMS Collingwood

Naval gunnery practice

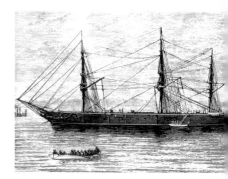

HMS Devastation

HMS Warrior

Torpedo drill on HMS Inflexible, 1891

In 1860, the first ironclad, HMS *Warrior* was launched, a new vessel built entirely of iron, not just with iron over wood. Others came into service but they still used sails until the appearance of HMS *Devastation* in 1873. She was the first modern warship. She had an iron hull, a screw, no sails and guns in turrets instead of in the old broadside arrangement. Invention of a breech-block made it possible to give up muzzle-loading, while high explosive shells replaced cannon balls. By 1877, torpedoes had come into use and a new type of warship, the destroyer, was introduced to deal with torpedo-boats.

As for the crews, the bad old custom of forcing men into the Service by press gangs came to an end in 1853. From then on, volunteers could sign on for a career in the Navy. A regular uniform for naval seamen came into use in 1857.

13 Wars in Queen Victoria's Reign

Uniform of the 13th Light Infantry in 1848

Florence Nightingale in a Crimean hospital

Since William IV's reign British soldiers had worn red coats, with white or blue trousers and a tall cap called a shako, though the Guards wore bearskins. The cavalry, known as dragoons and hussars, wore even handsomer uniforms and were armed with lances, sabres and long pistols, called carbines.

The wars in Queen Victoria's reign were fought far from Britain, and disturbed little, if at all, the life of the ordinary citizen. The Crimean War, in which Florence Nightingale won fame, was fought against Russia on the shores of the Black Sea. The Indian Mutiny caused the British Government to take over the rule of India from the East India Company.

In these wars foot-soldiers were armed with the rifle, which was still muzzle-loaded. The soldier bit off the end of a paper cartridge, poured the gunpower down the barrel, and rammed home the wad and the bullet. For charges and all close work the bayonet was fixed to the rifle.

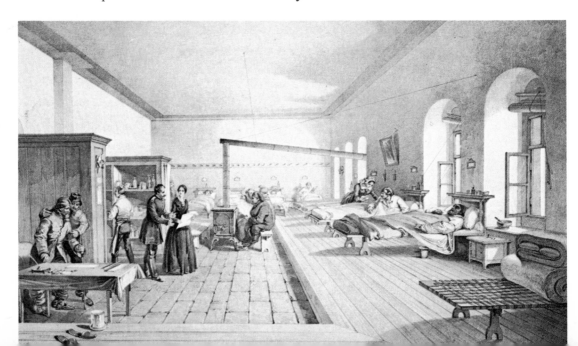

The Boer War

A Gatling gun

Cannons were now known as field-guns or artillery. They fired grape shot against troops, and cannon balls against forts and buildings. These tore holes in the walls, but did not explode like modern shells.

By the Boer War, against the Dutch settlers in South Africa, rifles had been introduced which were loaded at the breech instead of at the muzzle. The barrel was grooved, causing the bullet to spin as it passed through. This made shooting more accurate than firing through a plain tube. The first machine-guns, called Gatlings, were also in use at this time; so, too, were explosive shells, balloons, searchlights and despatch-riders on bicycles. This was the last war in which cavalry was widely used with success.

Dragoon Guard, 1855

Khaki, which was already in use in India, became the colour of uniforms in wartime, for in a dry and dusty country it made soldiers more difficult to see. The splendid uniforms of scarlet and gold, with gleaming helmets and plumes were reserved for special occasions in peace-time.

The simple warfare when two armies formed up and marched towards each other in broad daylight and fought, while the generals watched the battle from a short distance away had vanished. Modern warfare was coming, with all its terrible weapons, aimed not only at soldiers and sailors, but against ordinary men, women and children.

Infantry of the
Crimean War period

14 The Post

A post boy of the 18th century

A Victorian letterbox

In Tudor times royal messengers and the servants of great men carried letters and despatches for their masters to all parts of the kingdom. Charles I and the Stuarts allowed people to use the royal service of post-horses if they paid a fee when the letter was delivered. The letters were merely folded and sealed with a blob of wax. Even as early as 1660 post-dates were stamped on letters.

William Dockwra started a private Penny Post in London in 1680. It was so successful that it was very soon taken over as part of the royal service, and the fees for letters made up a useful part of the king's income.

By Georgian days, the post-boys who carried the mails proved lazy and dishonest. They were replaced by the famous mail-coaches, which ran on regular routes to and from Lombard Street in London, with the mail-bags in the charge of the guard. The cost of sending a letter depended on the distance it had to travel. As the fee was often high, people began to dodge payment by giving letters and messages to coachmen to deliver privately.

Clerks were used to copy documents

Typewriters began to replace handwriting for business letters

The first letterbox, 1855

Rowland Hill discovered a satisfactory way out of this difficulty. In 1840 he started the Penny Post. A letter cost a penny for each half ounce, no matter how far it had to travel. The letter was paid for when posted, instead of on arrival, and this led to the use of postage stamps and envelopes. The first British stamp bore the head of the young Queen Victoria, and was called the Penny Black.

Telegrams

Telegraphy, the method of passing messages along an electrified wire, was invented by an Englishman named Wheatstone and improved by Samuel Morse in America. The first telegraph service was installed in 1838 on the London and Blackwall Railway. As the railways spread all over England, telegraph poles were erected alongside the tracks.

Messages could now be sent in a few minutes to distant places, whereas, not so very long before, it had taken a messenger on horseback several days to reach them. Today we have become so used to the idea of speed that it is difficult to realise how very wonderful this invention seemed to the Victorians.

The telephone

Somewhat later, in 1876, telephones were invented by Alexander Graham Bell, a Scotsman who settled in Boston, America. At first they were expensive and people were slow to have these strange instruments installed. By 1900 only 10 000 were in use in Britain. The Electric Telegraph Company and the National Telephone Company, which operated these useful services in their early days, were eventually taken over by the Post Office.

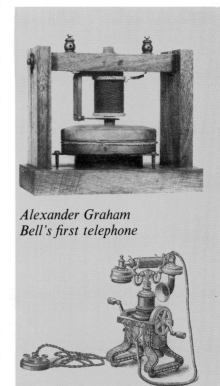

Alexander Graham Bell's first telephone

A telephone of 1892

15 Poor People in Victorian Days

A mudlark

Carrying coal to the surface—a job done by women

Children at work

In the first half of Queen Victoria's long reign there were a great many poor people in London and the big factory towns. Hordes of ragged, dirty children were to be seen in the streets, earning a living as best they could. Little boys and girls, hoping for a halfpenny, rushed to sweep the road clean for any lady or gentleman wishing to cross the muddy highway, and others held bridles of waiting horses for a penny.

By the Thames, lads called 'mudlarks' waded at low tide in the filthy mud, searching for scraps of iron and lead to sell. Hundreds of these ragged urchins had never been to school or had a good meal in their lives. They spent their days picking and stealing, to make a few pence to take home to their families living in tumbledown houses and miserable alleys.

Crossing sweepers

Second-hand clothes shop

There were many children who had no homes at all. They slept among barrows in the great markets or under railway bridges. They begged for food or searched dustbins for scraps to eat.

In the factory towns at this time, children of six and seven years old worked at machines from early in the morning until evening, for a few pence each week. The hours were so long that many fell asleep from weariness. Their mothers worked twelve and fourteen hours a day, too, yet there was seldom enough to eat at home, and certainly little warmth or clothing.

Orphans from the workhouse were housed by the factory owner in the 'prentice house, where they slept in shifts. This means that one set of children were in bed while another set were working. They spent nearly all their waking hours at work. There was no holiday on Saturday and part of Sunday was spent cleaning the machines.

Women and children worked down the coalmines. They pushed the coal-trucks, or sat for hours in the darkness working the ventilation doors, or crawled along on all fours like animals, harnessed to a truck with a chain.

All this unhappiness and poverty puzzled kindly people when they learned about it from a book published in 1842. But even so, many of them thought that such things could not be avoided and were even necessary. 'The poor,' they said 'are ever with us.'

One tap served many families

Children working in a coal mine

The miner's bath

'Flowers, penny a bunch!'

Muffin man

Street life

A man called Henry Mayhew went into the poorest parts of London to find out for himself how the people lived, and afterwards he wrote a book about all he had seen.

He discovered that the poorest people of all lived in slums called 'rookeries' which were clusters of tumble-down, ancient houses built round filthy courts and alleys. The people who lived there, workmen, pedlars, beggars and thieves, had many odd ways of making their living.

First, there were the costermongers, who sold fruit, vegetables and other things from their donkey-barrows. They were rough, lively men, dressed in corduroys with pearly buttons. They were fond of gambling, singing and fighting, but they were kind to their bulldogs and donkeys.

A costermonger

A coffee stall

Then there were hordes of street-sellers who cried out their wares in the streets: sellers of fly-papers; walking-sticks and whips; pipes, snuff and tobacco boxes; old clothes. All these and many other odd things were sold all day long: needles and spoons; boiled puddings; cakes, tarts, gingerbread; hot green peas; dogs' meat; pea-soup and hot eels; live animals and birds; watercress.

Other less respectable tradesmen were: old clothes men, rabbit-skin buyers, rag-pickers, and sewer-hunters, who entered the London sewers at low tide and searched the ancient, dangerous tunnels for anything of value.

There were dog-stealers who carried a bag into which they popped any good-looking dog. Later on, they claimed a reward from the owner, for 'finding' it.

Some of the cries were:

'Fresh watercresses!'
'Ha'penny, half-pint, milk. O!'
'Here's all hot! Here's all hot!' (pies)
'Catch 'em alive, only a ha'penny!' (fly-papers)
'Oysters, penny a lot!'

There were also large numbers of wandering workmen who called at respectable houses or shouted their trade in every street. There were scissors-grinders, chair-menders, mat-menders, rat-catchers, shoe-blacks and chimney-sweeps. Every chimney-sweep had his boy who, brush in hand, was forced to climb up inside the chimneys.

Rat catcher and long-song seller

'Cats' and dogs' meat!'

Nightmen, who cleaned out cess-pits

At this time, just over one hundred years ago, when Dickens was living in London and writing his books, street-musicians were to be seen and heard every day. There was the German band, the Italian hurdy-gurdy man with his monkey in a little red cap, the barrel-organ grinder, the ballad singer and the one-man band, in which one man played several instruments at the same time. He had pan-pipes in his mouth, a drum on his back, which he beat with a stick tied to his elbow, cymbals on top of the drum, clashed by means of a string tied to one heel, and a triangle in his hand!

There were jugglers, Punch and Judy shows, stilt walkers, performing dogs and dancing bears. Lastly, those with nothing to sell and no tricks to perform begged for a living. Foreigners who came to London, the richest city in the world in those days, were horrified at the large number of beggars in every street and thoroughfare.

A one-man band

Child selling wallflowers in the street

Punch and Judy

80

There were two more entertainments to be seen any day in the London streets: the evening newspaper boy on his penny-farthing bicycle, scorching through the traffic and between the horse-buses at breakneck speed, and the fire-engine, drawn by two galloping grey horses, clearing its way, not by a bell, but by the yelling of its entire crew.

London Bridge in the rush hour

The fire engine

South Wales in the 1880s

Lord Shaftesbury visiting a coal mine

Lord Shaftesbury

Lord Shaftesbury was the leader of a group of men and women who were ashamed that children were forced to work long hours in factories and coalmines. When he tried to persuade Parliament to forbid children working more than 10 hours a day, he was told that such a law would ruin the country and the cotton trade of Lancashire.

But he refused to give in, and at last Parliament agreed that children under 13 years old must not work more than eight hours a day, and women and children must no longer be sent underground to work in the mines. Rules were made for factories, and inspectors were sent round to see that they were obeyed.

It was some time before very much notice was taken of the new laws, but gradually throughout Queen Victoria's reign working conditions improved, especially for poor children.

Following Lord Shaftesbury's example, many clergymen, preachers and ladies from well-to-do families, of whom Florence Nightingale is the most famous, began to help the poor. These splendid men and women spent their lives trying to improve a world which had grown hard and cruel.

The Victorians 16

Design for a wrought iron gate

Houses

The builders of Queen Anne's reign and of Georgian days knew how to build a house which was handsome and pleasing in proportion. During Victorian days, a great many houses, especially middle-class villas, were badly designed and grossly over-decorated. Perhaps in the haste to make money there was no time for beauty and good taste in buildings, furniture and pictures, or perhaps the people who could not see the misery of the poor, and the ugliness of the factory towns, were just as blind to fair and shapely things.

If a picture, a chair or a house is badly shaped, it cannot be improved afterwards by putting on a lot of fancy and unnecessary decoration. Yet this is exactly what many Victorian builders tried to do. Their houses were ugly in shape, and every kind of pinnacle, turret, balcony and iron railing was added.

A Victorian parlour

A design for a porch

A Victorian 'Gothic' villa

83

A Victorian villa and a terrace in Leamington

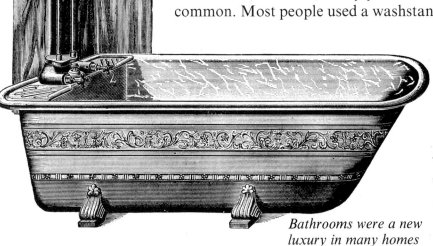

Another popular fashion of the time was the building of imitation castles and vast hideous country houses in the Gothic style of churches and cathedrals of the later Middle Ages. The 'new-Gothic' style was an imitation of the glorious arches and spires of the Middle Ages, and quite unsuitable for houses.

Although there were many curious houses built at this time, not all Victorian houses were like this. And even though their outside appearance may have been unpleasing, inside they were beginning to include conveniences such as bathrooms, lavatories and hot water systems, which in former days had existed only in a very few homes of the rich. It was, however, many years before bathrooms were common. Most people used a washstand in their bedroom.

Bathrooms were a new luxury in many homes

Gas-lighting indoors became general, and in many homes remained in use until after the Second World War. Gas cookers were on show in the 1851 exhibition, but most Victorian houses were fitted with the kitchen range, which had taken the place of the open fire. In its day the range was a great advance on any other stove. There was the fire in the centre and an oven on one side, heated by hot air, and a water tank on the other side, with a tap from which hot water could be drawn off.

A wringer

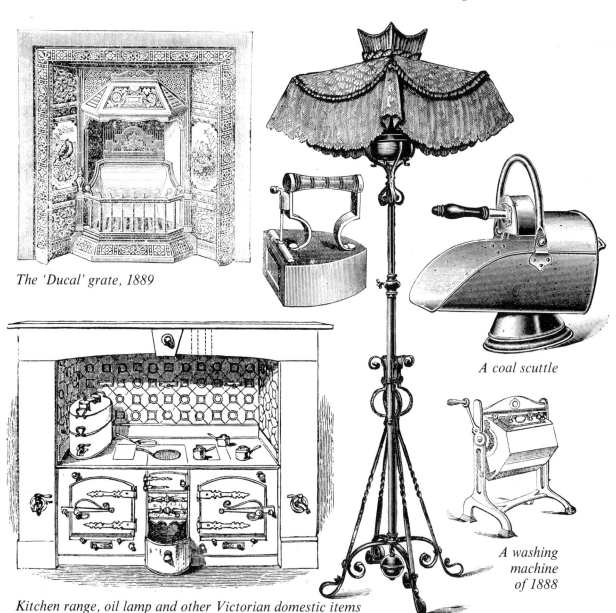

The 'Ducal' grate, 1889

A coal scuttle

A washing machine of 1888

Kitchen range, oil lamp and other Victorian domestic items

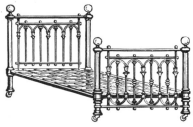

Very Handsome Black and Brass French
Bedstead.
Superior Finish.

Bedroom furniture

Table lamp

Furniture

Much Victorian furniture suffered from the same faults as the houses. The grace of Heppelwhite and Chippendale furniture was replaced by fussy furniture with far too much ornament, and it was usually made of mahogany, brass or iron.

People with plenty of money often had homes crowded with furniture. Never were rooms so cluttered up with chairs, tables, occasional tables, plant pot stands, over-mantels, pianos, bookcases, fretwork and strange pieces called 'whatnots'.

Windows were heavily draped with lace curtains and inner curtains of heavy material. Tables were covered with cloths with fringes and bobbles round the edges, and even the piano legs were given frills. Huge pictures in velvet frames and dark photographs of the whole family covered the walls, while shelves and china cabinets were laden with vases, plants and wax fruit under glass cases.

Clothes in Victorian days

At the beginning of Victoria's reign ladies wore a great many clothes: five or six petticoats under dresses of silk and taffeta. Waists were so tiny that ladies often fainted because their corsets were laced too tightly. Poke bonnets and shawls were fashionable. Dresses for dance or ball were low-cut, leaving the shoulders bare.

About 1845

In the middle of the reign came the crinoline, a full hooped petticoat, which expanded the skirt worn over it. Next came the bustle, a pad or cushion worn at the back, just below the waist line, to make a lady's skirt stand out behind. Later, dresses with leg-of-mutton sleeves were fashionable, and muffs and fans reappeared.

About 1865

Men's clothes became quieter in colour, and a neck-cloth tied in a knot was worn instead of collars and ties. Almost every Victorian gentleman wore a beard or moustache, though some preferred side-whiskers called mutton-chops and Dundrearies. Beards came back into fashion during the Crimean War, in imitation of the soldiers. Cigarettes also appeared at this time, for the soldiers copied this manner of smoking from the Turkish troops.

Towards the end of Victoria's reign men's clothes became more and more like our present-day style, except that trousers were tighter and top hats and bowler hats were worn by almost everybody. Quite humble clerks went to the office every morning in a topper, and only costers and cads at the Derby wore caps.

Straw boaters were fashionable in summer for both ladies and gentlemen

About 1840   *The crinoline, about 1860*

A dame school in Camden Town. An old lady taught a few village children in her cottage. Local people gave a small sum of money for this work

Flogging was part of the life of many schools

Schools

For many years schools of various kinds had existed, but there were very few for the children of poor parents. The great Public Schools such as Eton, Harrow and Rugby had become expensive schools for children of the well-to-do. There were also the old Grammar Schools, many of them dating back to the time of Edward VI and Elizabeth. To these went the sons of merchants and citizens who were able to pay the fees.

Many children of wealthy parents did not go to school at all, but were taught by a governess or tutor in the schoolrooms of their big houses.

Girls' schools were few in number. They taught deportment (how to walk and sit gracefully), manners, needlework, dancing and a little music and reading. For the most part, girls were expected to learn at home how to run a house, how to cook and how to make preserves and jams, wines and simple medicines.

There were also many children who worked in factories and had no time for schooling. Christian men and women were distressed that these boys and girls were growing up ignorant of Jesus Christ and unable to read and write. They started Sunday Schools and Church Day Schools. Sometimes children already at work came to school for part of the day. By the time Victoria became Queen, the Government had begun to help build schools for working-class children.

As a result of Lord Shaftesbury's Factory Acts, children now had time for school. In 1870 Parliament insisted that every child must go to school from the age of five until thirteen, and that parents must pay a little—six or nine pence a week—towards the cost.

Many schools were now built. These were called Board Schools, because they were managed by a Board, or Committee, of Managers. Those built by the Churches were usually known as National Schools. Nowadays these schools would be considered very dull places indeed. Classes of 60 or 80 children had one teacher, who was helped by a young pupil-teacher, apprenticed for five years to learn teaching.

In some schools it was the custom for 'monitors', older children, to teach the younger children in groups arranged round the walls of a large room. The monitors pointed to letters and words, and the children recited them aloud. The Schoolmaster sat at a high desk to keep order. He was very strict and often used the cane. Lessons were usually Scripture, reading, writing and arithmetic.

At first, parents were very angry that their children had to go to school instead of earning money, and when builders came to put up a school in the slums, they were chased away!

A Ragged School

Board Schools provided education for the kind of life they expected their pupils to lead

At the piano

Papa and Mama

Family life

Victorian family life

During the reign of Queen Victoria there was much poverty and misery, but for middle-class families it was a time of happy family life. Their way of life and many of their ideas may seem strange to us and often rather hard, but the Victorians were contented, and they were satisfied with few pleasures.

Father, known as Papa, was the head of the house, and everyone, especially the children, treated him with the greatest respect. His word was law for all the household: his wife, children and servants. He sat at the head of the table and carved the great joint of meat at dinner, and the youngsters were not supposed to talk unless spoken to by a grown-up.

Mama kept her large family in order, and used a penny cane, if necessary. With eight, ten, twelve or more children, she was a very busy mother, for there were no vacuum-cleaners, washing-machines or electrical gadgets in the house. Tinned goods and foods prepared in packets were unknown. Clothes were mostly made at home or at a dressmaker's in the town. After she was 30 years of age, Mama was considered quite middle-aged and often took to wearing a little lace cap in the house.

Each morning, Papa took family prayers, when everyone, including the servants knelt down in the dining-room or study. He also led the family to church on Sunday morning and again in the evening, when they sat in the family pew.

Sunday was a very solemn day and as little work as possible was done. No shops were open and there were certainly no amusements. Everyone put on their best clothes, which were usually stiff and uncomfortable. On Sunday afternoons the family often went for a walk, but no games with a ball or hoop were allowed. Even picture books were forbidden on Sundays; Sunday reading included the Bible and certain books about the saints and the missionaries.

The nineteenth century was a time of emigration from the overcrowded island and it was common for younger sons of these large families to go overseas to find work and to make their homes in Canada, Australia and New Zealand. Many, especially the Scots and the Irish, went to America.

Church on Sunday

The village choir

Cheap imported food was available at the end of the century

A music hall

The adventures and discoveries of such men as David Livingstone and H M Stanley, and later Cecil Rhodes, fired the imaginations of young men at home, and they set off to make their fortunes. Cargoes of cheap grain and meat coming from new lands across the sea ruined many British farmers, and this caused hundreds of farm workers to try their luck in the colonies.

Although there were no radios, television, cinemas or motor-cars, the Victorians did not find life dull. People worked longer hours, often 12 or 14 hours a day. Shops opened before breakfast and stayed open until 9 o'clock at night and 11 pm on Saturdays. Half-days and annual holidays were rare, and shop assistants usually had to 'live in' above the shop.

Astley's Circus

Amusements were simple and the family often gathered round the piano to sing the latest popular songs, or they entertained each other by reciting or playing the piano. Public readings from Dickens and recitations were popular, drawing large audiences. In London and the large towns the music-halls were considered not quite respectable, but the theatre was sometimes visited.

Children very rarely went to any entertainment, except perhaps to the circus or to a pantomime. They had their parties, with many games which we still play today: hunt the slipper, postman's knock, blind man's buff. Comics and magazines were less common in those days. The best known were *The Boys' Own Paper, The Girls' Own Paper* and *Little Folks*.

A dolls' house used by Queen Victoria as a child

A tennis party

Croquet

Books they had in plenty, but the pictures and covers were often dull. Many of the best children's stories were written in Victorian days, including *Alice in Wonderland, The Water Babies, Tom Brown's Schooldays, Black Beauty, Little Women* and *Treasure Island.* There were books of adventure by R M Ballantyne, Jules Verne, G A Henty and Captain Marryat.

Children's games had mysterious 'seasons': hoops, tops, marbles, hop-scotch came in and went out at their proper times. Battledore and shuttlecock, and an amusing game called diabolo, were fashionable. Grown-ups as well as children played croquet, a game in which the ladies' long skirts were less of a nuisance than at tennis.

International football —England v. Scotland at Sheffield, 1882

At cricket the first Test Match was played in 1882, and the Football League was formed six years later. It was common for footballers to play with caps on.

Toys were not so varied and splendid as they are today. It was the time of the rocking-horse and Noah's Ark, of the wax-faced doll and boxes of tin and lead soldiers. Magic lanterns, which threw pictures on to a screen, were a great novelty, and so were model steam-engines with real boilers which were heated by methylated spirit.

At the end of the old Queen's long reign, Britain was the richest country on earth. Her ships sailed to the corners of the world, taking goods from her factories and bringing back gold, corn, frozen meat and every kind of food and luxury for rich and poor.

Britain controlled a great part of the world's trade and ruled the biggest Empire ever known. People, even the poor, were proud of their country and Empire. They sang patriotic songs, believed in progress and thought that the British had a special mission to manage most of the world's affairs and to rule over millions of people in distant lands.

In 1901 the Queen died, after a reign of 64 years. Jovial Edward VII became king and everyone looked forward to peace and plenty.

Queen Victoria in her old age

Wealthy boys home for the school holidays

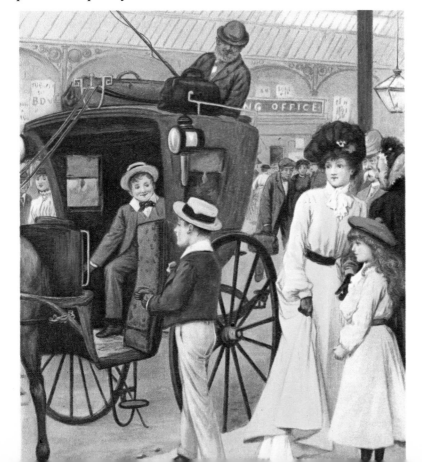

95

Index

Looking at History   R J Unstead

A car of 1924

Book Five

The Twentieth Century

Adam and Charles Black   London

Acknowledgements

Aerofilms Ltd   43, 44a
Brighton Public Library   8d
British Aircraft Corporation   28c
British Airways   25a, 28b
British Broadcasting Corporation   32c, 33b & c, 34a & b
British Petroleum   59c
British Rail   54c, 55a, b, c & d, 56a, b, c & d
Lance Browne   46b
Crown Copyright: Central Office of Information   59b, 60b
Cunard Ltd   59a
Walt Disney Productions Ltd   52a
Dunlop Ltd   cover
English Rose Kitchens Ltd   50c
Mary Evans Picture Library   2, 3, 7a & b, 8a & b, 9a, 10a,
    11b, 13b, 14b, 15b, 17c & d, 19a, 23a & c, 30c, 35b, 36b,
    38a, 40b, 41a, 42b, 47a, b, c & d, 48a, b & c, 50a & b, 57c,
    60a, 62a and title page
Hoverlloyd Ltd   29b
Imperial War Museum   57a
Infoplan Ltd   6b
Knight Lloyd Burnham Ltd   61a, b, c & d, 62b
London Transport   12a & c
Manchester Central Library   63b
Mander and Mitchenson Collection   51a & b, 52b & c
Mansell Collection   10b
National Motor Museum   8c, 11a, 13a
Radio Times Hulton Picture Library   5b, 16a, 17a, 18c,
    19b & c, 20a, b & c, 20e, 22a & b, 30a & b, 31a & b, 32a,
    36a, 37a, 39a & b, 42a, 53a, b & c
Raleigh Industries Ltd   16b & c
Rowntree Mackintosh Ltd   38b
Leo di Salvo   20d
Shuttleworth Collection   24c, 27a
Unilever Ltd   42c
United States Information Service   6a
Westland Helicopters Ltd   29a
F White   27b
P F White   9c, 13c, 14a, 15a, 32b, 41b, c & d, 42d, 44b, c & d,
    45a, b & c, 46a, 46c, 63a
Drawings are by Doreen Roberts

Published by A & C Black (Publishers) Ltd
35 Bedford Row, London WC1R 4JH

ISBN 0 7136 1443 9 limp
     0 7136 1444 7 net

First published 1974. Reprinted 1976, 1978 & 1979
© 1974 A & C Black Ltd

Printed in Great Britain by Sir Joseph Causton & Sons Ltd,
London and Eastleigh

Paris fashion, 1914

Contents

Trains at Dover Station in 1903

Some of the chief events 1

1901 Accession of Edward VII. A 1000-mile race for motor cars in Britain. Marconi sent wireless signals across the Atlantic.
1902 End of Boer War. Ford's car plant, Detroit.
1903 Wright brothers' first aeroplane flight. *The Great Train Robbery*, pioneer film.
1908 First Model T Ford. Old Age Pensions in Britain.
1909 Blériot flew English Channel.
1910 Accession of George V.
1912 Scott's Antarctic expedition.

1914–18 The First World War
Germany invaded Belgium; trench warfare. In Eastern Europe, Russia was attacked by Germany and Austria. 1915 Gallipoli. 1916 First use of tanks. Verdun. Jutland. 1917 U-boat campaign. Russian Revolution. America entered war. 1918 German surrender.

1919 Versailles Peace Conference. Alcock and Brown flew the Atlantic.
1920 First Meeting of the League of Nations.
1921 Independence of Southern Ireland.
1922 Broadcasting started in London.
1926 Baird demonstrated television. General strike in Britain.
1927 First talkie films.
1929 Penicillin discovered.
1933 Hitler Chancellor of Germany.
1936 *Queen Mary's* maiden voyage. First public television programme. Edward VIII abdicated. Accession of George VI.

Edward VII

Scott's ship in the Antarctic

Astronauts on the surface of the moon

1939–45 The Second World War
Nazi Germany attacked Poland; 1940 overran Norway, Belgium, Holland, France. Italy joined Germany. The British Commonwealth fought on alone. Battle of Britain. 1941 Hitler attacked Russia. Japan destroyed US fleet at Pearl Harbour, captured Singapore, America entered war. 1942 Alamein, Stalingrad. 1943 Allies invaded Italy. 1944 Normandy landings. Russian victories. 1945 Germany surrendered. Japan surrendered after dropping of atomic bomb.

1946 First meeting of United Nations Organisation.
1947 India and Pakistan became independent.
1948 Transistor radios and LP records introduced.
1950 Korean War. United Nations army in action.
1951 Festival of Britain.
1952 Accession of Elizabeth II. First hydrogen bomb.
1953 Everest climbed. Death of Stalin.
1956 Suez Canal taken by President Nasser of Egypt.
1957 Ghana first British colony in Africa to become independent. Russian Sputnik launched into space.
1958 Fuchs crossed Antarctic.
1961 South Africa left the Commonwealth. Yuri Gagarin first man into space.
1963 President Kennedy assassinated.
1965 Vietnam war began.
1967 *Queen Elizabeth II* launched.
1969 Armstrong and Aldrin landed on moon. *Concorde*'s maiden flight.
1973 Britain entered the European Community, or Common Market.

The Bahamas Independence ceremony in 1973. Many Commonwealth countries have become independent of Britain since 1945

6

Road transport 2

Daimler car of 1892

Motor cars

In Britain, the Red Flag Act of 1862 drove steam-coaches off the roads, because a man carrying a red flag had to walk in front of a 'horseless carriage'. Maximum speed was to be 2 mph. This made steam vehicles so slow that they could not compete with horse-drawn traffic.

On the Continent, where there was no such law, French and German engineers were able to go on with their experiments. One of their main problems was to build a vehicle light enough not to break up the roads.

It is generally agreed that a German named Karl Benz built the first petrol-driven 'car' in 1885. This was a tricycle with a $\frac{3}{4}$ hp (horse-power) engine at the back. Two years later, another German, Gottlieb Daimler, constructed the first Daimler car. Both men had found that a petrol engine could be built lighter than a steam engine.

After these first cars had appeared, others developed rapidly, especially in France, where a firm called Panhard & Levassor obtained permission to use Daimler engines. In 1888 they built over 100 cars. At Detroit in America, Henry Ford produced his first car in 1893, a 2-cylinder 4 hp model.

Panhard & Levassor car of 1894

Benz three-wheeler of 1888 (left) and the first Ford, 1896 (right)

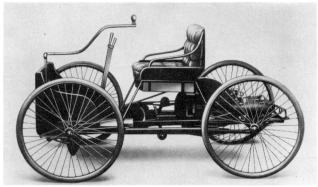

7

Meanwhile, British engineers were still hampered by the Red Flag Act, but in 1895 a rich enthusiast brought back a Panhard car from France. Others followed his example and a motor-show was held at Tunbridge Wells, where Panhard and Peugeot cars, a De Dion steam-car and a Daimler motor-cycle aroused great interest.

This event led to the abolition of the Red Flag Act and the speed limit was raised to 14 mph. To celebrate this new freedom and to demonstrate the speed and reliability of motor-cars, a run was arranged in 1896 from London to Brighton. Nearly 50 cars set out and 13 completed the 53-mile journey.

The first British-built car was a Lanchester; Daimler cars began to be made at Coventry.

A delivery van of 1897 and a 12 hp De Dion of 1904

These early cars were steered by a tiller. Engine speed was controlled by a hand-lever, the wheels had solid tyres and the brakes, made from wooden or leather blocks, were far from reliable. There were no roofs or windscreens, so motorists wore thick coats, gauntlets and goggles, while lady passengers put on veils to protect their faces from clouds of dust raised by the wheels.

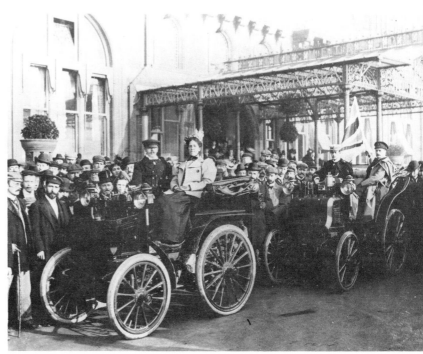

The London-Brighton rally of 1896 (right) and in the 1970s (above)

A car crash in 1900 (left) and a Swift car of 1905 (above)

Motorists felt themselves to be pioneers, taking part in an exciting form of sport. Since there were no filling-stations or repair depots, they had to carry spare cans of petrol and spare tyres and to be ready to carry out repairs by the roadside. They also had to stand a good deal of ridicule from the public and hostility from drivers of horse-drawn vehicles who complained that the noise and frequent explosions from cars frightened their horses. Since motoring was an expensive hobby, only rich enthusiasts could afford to own a car.

This hotel, built about 1900, wanted to attract motorists as well as people with horsedrawn carriages

By 1910, cars had begun to take on the shape which is familiar to us today. They were still roofless and much higher off the road, but they now had windscreens, steering-wheels, gear-boxes, brass headlamps and pneumatic tyres made by Dunlop or Michelin.

These air-filled tyres sucked dust up from the roads and made driving unpleasant for motorists and everyone else until the problem was solved by spraying the road surfaces with tar.

ALL the joy of motoring is materially increased by the knowledge that in your sturdy Overland you have all the Elegance, Luxury and Reliability that has ever been incorporated in *any* Motor vehicle, regardless of cost . . . .

DYNAMO LIGHTING
SELF-STARTER

£275

IMMEDIATE DELIVERY.

WILLYS OVERLAND LTD., 151-153 GT. PORTLAND ST., LONDON, W.

An advertisement of 1914

Chain driven Humber motor bicycle

Numbers of small firms were now making cars, building each one separately by hand. Besides Lanchesters and Daimlers, makes such as Humber, Riley, Lagonda, Sunbeam, Swift, Napier and Singer appeared on British roads. The new king, Edward VII, was himself a keen motorist; his example encouraged others to try the sport.

Racing was introduced. In 1902, a 40 hp Napier won at 36 mph, while in the following year, a Mercedes reached the record speed of 49 mph.

Various motor-cycles made their appearance, some with a side-car for a passenger. To start his machine, the driver had to run hard, pushing it along until the engine fired, and then leap on to the saddle..

A road race in France, 1907

10

A 1909 Model T Ford

1915 Ford advertisement. Prices quoted were: Runabout £125 Touring car £135 Town 'landaulette' £185 Delivery van £130

In America, Henry Ford hit on a method of making cars more cheaply, so that people of moderate means could afford to buy them. He designed a sturdy reliable car that would travel over the bad roads of the time and he produced it in large numbers by what came to be called mass-production methods. Car parts, such as body, seats and engine, were made by various firms and assembled at Ford's plant. Workers concentrated on one job only, such as bolting on the wheels, and this resulted in the cars being built more quickly and cheaply, especially as there was only one type. This was the famous Model T Ford, soon to be known all over the world as the 'Tin Lizzie'. The first one appeared in 1908, costing $525 or about £175 and, by 1915, over a million were on the roads.

An Englishman named William Morris (afterwards Lord Nuffield) went to America to study Ford's methods but his plan to produce cheaper cars in England had to be postponed when war broke out in 1914.

*Trams at Tooting,
London, in 1911*

*One of London's last
horse buses (top) and
a trolley-bus of 1931*

Buses and trams

Meanwhile, the ordinary man's best chance of riding in a motor-vehicle was to use a bus. As early as 1905, the London General Omnibus Company started converting its horse-buses by fitting petrol-engines to them. For a while, they still had iron-rimmed wheels and the top deck was open to the weather. For outings, the horse-drawn 'charabanc' began to be replaced by an open-top motor coach which could be covered in by a hood when it rained.

London and most large towns were also served by trams, usually double-deckers, which ran on rails let into the roadway. These had been developed in the 19th century and they came into widespread use during the early years of the present century. Power was supplied from overhead electric cables, though some systems used a live cable in a slot in the road.

Trams running on fixed tracks proved to be a nuisance as traffic increased and, by the 1950s, most tramway systems had been scrapped. In some places, trolley-buses, using overhead cables, replaced the trams but these too have mostly disappeared.

Cars since 1918

Production of private motor cars practically ceased during the 1914–18 War but, when peace came, Morris and another Englishman, Herbert Austin, were able to produce cars by methods similar to Henry Ford's.

In the 1920s and 30s the cost of motoring came down and down. People who were moderately well-off could buy an Austin Seven for about £165, a 'bull-nosed' Morris Cowley for £340 or a Morris Minor for only £125. More luxurious models included the Bentley, the Rolls-Royce, the Sunbeam and the Rover.

1930 Hillman advertisement

A 1928 4½ litre Bentley (top) and an Austin Seven of the 1930s

13

Garages are now an ugly part of our scenery. Their huge signs are meant to be read from a distance

1934 Morris advertisement. The Morris Ten-Four saloon cost £175

As lively as a surf-board .... these new Morris cars

.... yet understandingly responsive to the slightest touch of control. Fast enough to satisfy the youngest summer sports enthusiast .... power in plenty .... buoyant riding comfort that leaves you fresh after the hardest, hottest day .... roof and windows that open to the sun and air without hair-ruffling draughts .... silent synchromesh gears that slide so deftly into place .... *and the secret of all this is Balanced Motoring — that carefully planned combination of perfectly matched qualities found in every Morris car.*

MORRIS
The car you're proud to own

MORRIS TEN-FOUR SALOON (sliding head) £175 • OTHER MODELS from 8 to 25 h.p. from £110-£395

Car-racing aroused enormous interest between the wars when British drivers like Sir Henry Segrave broke the world record with 231 mph in 1929, while Sir Malcolm Campbell reached over 300 mph in 1935.

The design of racing cars influenced ordinary road models, so that they became more streamlined; mud-guards were incorporated into the body, running-boards vanished, brakes and gear-boxes were greatly improved. Other improvements like windscreen-wipers, heaters and indicators have made motoring safer and more comfortable.

As in 1914–18, the Second World War saw a drastic reduction in private motoring, but after the war came a tremendous rise in production. Since 1945, car manufacture has become one of Britain's major industries and cars of every type, size and price are turned out by the million.

The car has changed people's lives perhaps more than any other invention. People can now live far from their work; they can enjoy outings, travel and holidays which would have been beyond their grandfathers' dreams. Cars provide work for the thousands who make and sell and service them; they have altered the shape of houses and have changed the appearance of towns and countryside. They have also made crime much easier. Their fumes pollute the atmosphere and thousands of people are killed every year in car accidents.

Cars have altered the shape of our houses. Here the garages are underneath the living rooms

PUNCH, OR THE LONDON CHARIVARI.—November 6, 1929.

November Roads are 'Skiddy' Roads

A busy road scene in 1929. Notice the early traffic light and the outside steps on the back of the bus

15

Out for a spin in 1911

Bicycles

Bicycling had become a popular means of travel and also a sport in Victorian days. Early in the 20th century the bicycle entered its Golden Age. Edwardian roads were not choked with traffic, so the cyclist could speed along, happily overtaking horse-drawn vehicles and even the occasional motor car. Pneumatic tyres, introduced from 1888, and a sprung saddle gave him a more comfortable ride and he could climb hills more easily, thanks to the Sturmey-Archer 3-speed hub gear, patented in 1902.

Bicycles were not cheap at this time. A high-class model cost from £10 to £20 (equal to perhaps £100–£200 today); Raleigh, Sunbeam, Lea-Francis, Humber and Rudge were among the de-luxe makes and there was also the Dursley-Pederson 'Gentleman's Model Royal' at 16 or 18 guineas with 3-speed gear.

Cycling gave people the chance to travel to work more easily and to get out into the country. Club outings and holiday tours were popular and the Association of Cycle and Light-weight Campers, formed in 1909, had an enthusiastic membership. British racing cyclists dominated the world amateur sprint championships up to 1914, and W J Bailey alone won it four times.

For many years bicycle design showed little change, except that machines became lighter (from about 20 kilograms to 15 kilograms), owing to new types of steel, and lower, so that the rider could touch the ground with his feet while still seated.

In the 1940s and 50s, many cyclists fitted a small petrol-engine to drive the back wheel and to enable them to speed along without pedalling. This type is still seen on the Continent but in Britain it has been largely replaced by the scooter and the lightweight motor-cycle.

In 1962, a new bicycle appeared, the Moulton, with 40 cm diameter wheels in place of the usual 66 cm ones, and a special rubber suspension system. This novel machine brought new life to the cycle industry and led to the production of other types, such as the Triumph 'Twenty (20-inch) Shopper' for the housewives, the Sun 'Sporting 20', the 'RSW 14' and the 'Chopper' for youngsters.

Clothes 3

Hats on Brighton seafront in 1903

Dressmaker's dummy, 1909

Edwardian ladies wore skirts which swept the ground, often with trains that had to be held up when walking. Dresses were designed to create a stately figure with tiny waist, full bosom and shapely behind. Out of doors, three-quarter or half-length coats were popular, with huge hats, often decorated with plumes of feathers. A close-fitting hat called a *toque* was also worn.

For evening wear, the 'fine figure' of a woman was emphasised by draping the dress in spirals. Dresses were cut to give a 'sway back' impression, as though the lady was sticking her chest out while trying to prevent herself toppling forwards.

About 1910, skirts closed round the ankles so that the ladies could only walk in little mincing steps. This was the hobble skirt, to be followed some three years later by looser dresses rather like a Japanese kimono. Waists moved up high and some ladies daringly gave up wearing corsets.

Fashions of 1914

Men's clothes were mostly of formal cut and made in dark colours. Businessmen would wear a black morning coat with tails, narrow pin-stripe trousers, a stiff collar and a top hat or bowler. Trousers had turn-up bottoms and shoes were partly hidden by spats. These were short cloth gaiters which fastened round the ankle to cover the instep.

Clothes were mostly made by professional dress-makers, hats by milliners and gentlemen's suits by a bespoke tailor, for ready-made garments were looked down on as cheap and inferior. A clerk or a workman would buy a ready-made suit, known as a 'reach me down', but it would not fit well.

The poor relied on second-hand clothes from wardrobe shops and market barrows. Footwear was a real problem; a workman had to buy stout boots for work but his wife had to make do with second-hand shoes bought for a few pence, and the children often went barefoot in summer.

Gentleman wearing spats

Trying on a new overcoat, 1909

Second-hand shoe stall in London's East End

During the First World War, women took on men's work while their husbands and boy-friends were in the trenches. Trailing or hobble skirts would have been absurd garments in the factory or on the land, so skirts became wider and shorter—not much above the ankle, it is true, but for the first time for centuries, skirts rose above ground level.

Startling changes occurred in the 20s. Skirts rose almost to the knees, the waistline dropped to the hips and dresses were made straight down like tubes. Flesh-coloured stockings took the place of black ones; more women began wearing lipstick and make-up and they cut their hair short in the fashionable 'bob' or 'Eton crop'.

For a time, evening dresses were short in the front and longer at the back; then long dresses to the floor came back for dinners and dances but daytime skirts never returned to the ground until the 'maxi' dresses and coats of 1971.

A fashion of 1922

Women factory workers in 1916, polishing lenses

A group of office workers, 1928

19

The New Look of 1949 (left), slacks in the 1930s (centre) and leisurewear of 1936 (right)

During the 30s, women started wearing trousers at the seaside and in the country, and shorts for tennis. This was looked on as very modern and daring, but when the Second World War came, trousers were accepted as sensible wear in factories and on air-raid and rescue work.

After the war, women's clothes took on a more feminine shape for a time. The 'New Look', as it was called, produced long dresses and coats with small waists and flared skirts. This fashion gave way to more casual styles, with ever-shorter skirts until these eventually became 'mini'. Trousers, slacks and jeans have come back into fashion and, thanks to new materials and higher standards in ready-made garments, clothes are now cheaper and more varied than they have ever been.

Mini skirt, about 1970

Second-hand clothes stall, about 1950

Oxford bags

Sports jacket
and grey flannels

City pin-stripes

Brogue,
1930s

Chukka boot, 1947

Some hair and
whisker styles—late
Victorian, a 1950s
crew-cut, 1940s short
back and sides, and
1970 long hair and
beard. After 60 years,
beards came back
into fashion

1930 suit
with wide revers

1960 dinner-jacket
and dress shirt

Detachable starched
collar, 1925

Men's clothes have gradually become less formal. A sports jacket and flannel trousers at weekends made a pleasant change from the dark business suit and, between the wars, young men took to wearing plus-fours, baggy knicker-bockers which had been originally introduced for golf. Brown shoes replaced black and a coloured shirt with turned-down collar took the place of the white shirt and separate stiff or semi-stiff collar.

'Oxford bags', enormously wide trousers, had a vogue during the late twenties. Since then, trousers, like jacket revers (collars), have varied from narrow to very wide.

Plus-fours were
originally introduced
for golf

21

Colourful men's clothes of the 1970s

Wartime battledress probably gave men a liking for comfortable 'un-smart' wear; at all events, sweaters, slacks, jeans, round-necked shirts and anoraks now form a part of most men's wardrobes. Many garments are brightly-coloured and not confined to the blacks, browns and greys which used to be almost the only colours for men's wear. Nevertheless, 'dressing-up' has by no means died out; morning suits and top hats are still worn at some weddings and formal occasions. In the 40s and 50s, 'Teddy Boys' dressed themselves like Edwardian dandies; Italian styles were popular for a time and frilled shirts and brocaded waistcoats come back into favour from time to time. Styles have emerged for young men which are quite distinct from those worn by their fathers, and new fashions are always appearing.

A pre-war street scene would have shown four men out of five wearing a bowler, trilby hat or a cap, but hats are much less common nowadays.

Straw hats in 1931; and a Teddy Boy of 1954

22

Aircraft 4

The first powered flight took place in 1903 at Kitty Hawk, North Carolina, when two Americans, Wilbur and Orville Wright, managed to get off the ground for nearly a minute. Within two years, they had built an aeroplane which could turn, bank and stay up for half an hour.

This achievement aroused little interest in Europe until Wilbur Wright came over in 1908 to demonstrate his skill. Another American, 'Colonel' S F Cody, built a strange looking biplane and became the first man to fly in Britain.

When Louis Blériot, a French aviator, flew across the English Channel in 1909, his feat aroused enormous interest and prizes were offered for cross-country flights in which pioneers like Cody, Grahame-White and TOM Sopwith took part. The War Office realised that aircraft could play an important role in war, so the Royal Flying Corps was founded and trials and flying schools were introduced.

Blériot

Wilbur Wright with a lady passenger

The Wright brothers

Early aeroplanes were monoplanes (single-wing), biplanes and, occasionally, triplanes. The frames were made of wood (ash and spruce) with steel tubing for the undercarriage struts. Thin piano wire was used to brace the framework and this was covered with cotton or canvas, treated with liquid known as 'dope'. Crashes were not uncommon but pilots often escaped injury, because the frail structure would glide to earth with the wings taking the shock on landing.

The Vickers Vimy bomber in which Alcock and Brown crossed the Atlantic

Aeroplane design improved rapidly during the First World War, when machines like the Vickers Fighter, the Handley-Page Bomber and the Sopwith Camel came into service. By 1918 aircraft could climb to 9000 metres and had reached 250 km/h.

When the war ended, pilots turned their attention to civil flying, which meant pioneering the world's air routes. In 1918, Captain Ross Smith flew a Handley-Page Bomber from Cairo to India. In 1919 John Alcock and Arthur Brown, in a Vimy bomber, became the first men to fly the Atlantic. They left St John's, Newfoundland on 13 June and crash-landed at Clifden in Ireland 15 hours and 57 minutes later.

That same year, 1919, Captain Ross Smith and his brother Keith flew from London to Australia; the flight took nearly 28 days, owing to mishaps and bad weather. Accidents also delayed the first flight to South Africa in 1920, when Van Rynevald and Brand took 45 days to reach Capetown.

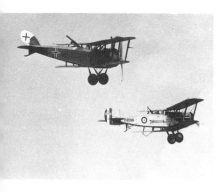

First World War fighters

Long-distance flying called for courage and resourcefulness, for there was no air control system or weather reports and not many landing grounds or experienced ground crews. Alan Cobham made his name in the 1920s for his flights to India, South Africa and Australia. In 1926, on his return from Australia, he made a spectacular landing in his seaplane on the River Thames beside the Houses of Parliament.

The American pilot, Charles Lindbergh became world famous when he made the first solo crossing of the Atlantic in 1927. Other celebrated pilots of this period were two Australians, Kingsford Smith and Bert Hinkler, a New Zealand girl, Jean Batten, and Amy Johnson, a girl from Hull in England, who flew alone to Australia.

These and many other pilots changed flying from high adventure into a routine method of transport. Companies were formed to carry passengers, mail and cargo. By the late 1930s, most of the world's major air routes had been established, though it was not yet possible for fare-paying passengers to make a direct crossing of the Atlantic by aeroplane.

An advertisement of the 1930s

Amy Johnson

The airship R101

Airships

Passengers could, however, cross the Atlantic by airship. The Germans had developed these great powered balloons before 1914, when Count von Zeppelin built several airships known as zeppelins. These were used to bomb London during the 1914–18 War and, later, to carry passengers.

The British airship *R34* crossed to New York and back as early as 1919 and ten years later, the German *Graf Zeppelin* flew round the world. This airship, over 230 metres long, flew at about 95 km/h, carrying a crew of 40 and some 20 passengers in great luxury. A regular trans-Atlantic service was established in the 30s, though the British had by then lost faith in airships after the *R101* crashed in France on her maiden flight to India. In 1937, a new German airship, the *Hindenburg* burst into flames at her moorings in New York and this disaster, together with the destruction of two American airships, put an end to this form of flying.

Airships were developed from balloons, such as this Montgolfier balloon of 1783

The Spitfire

Aeroplanes since 1939

The Second World War brought tremendous improvement in speed and performance of military aircraft, from the Spitfires and Hurricanes used in the Battle of Britain, the Wellington bombers, the American Flying Fortresses and Mustang fighters, to the German Junkers and Messerschmitt aircraft.

By the end of the war, aircraft powered by the jet-engine invented by Sir Frank Whittle were reaching speeds of 950 km/h. By 1949, the sound barrier had been broken, that is, aircraft had flown faster than the speed of sound, 1200 km/h.

A Sea Fury fighter with an aircraft carrier in the background

*A Comet airliner—
one of the first
passenger jets*

*Cargo being loaded on
a British Airways
Boeing 707*

*The Concorde comes
in to land*

Since that time, air travel has advanced by leaps and bounds; thousands of aircraft take off every day on scheduled flights throughout the world. Thanks to the development of radar (radio waves transmitted by ground stations and by aircraft as an aid to navigation and landing) a complex and wonderfully accurate system of control has been built up.

Aircraft have become bigger and faster with supersonic Jumbo-jets carrying passengers thousands of metres above the earth at speeds of over 1000 km/h. The Anglo-French Concorde was designed to carry 130 passengers across the Atlantic in $3\frac{1}{4}$ hours. The take-off noise made by these huge aircraft makes life unpleasant for people who live near airports and attempts are being made to produce quieter engines.

Helicopters, VTOL aircraft and hovercraft

An important type of aircraft which has been developed in recent years is the helicopter. Its origin was the *Autogyro*, produced by Juan de la Curva in 1923; this had a normal engine and propeller, but take-off was assisted by overhead rotor blades. Igor Sikorsky devised a power-driven rotor to lift the helicopter from the ground and also to propel it forwards and backwards and to enable it to hover.

Helicopters have proved immensely useful for inter-city travel, air-sea rescue work, aerial surveys and as air-ambulances to convey wounded from the battle areas.

The cost of providing enormous runways for aircraft take-off has led to the development of VTOL types (vertical take-off and landing). The Hawker-Siddeley Harrier uses nozzles which direct the thrust of the jet-engine downwards for take-off and this system may well be applied in the future to commercial aircraft.

Lastly, there is the hovercraft, an extraordinary machine invented by Sir Christopher Cockerell, which uses a down-thrust of air to form a cushion on which the broad flat hull of the craft is borne up, so it can skim across land or water. So far, in Britain, the hovercraft is mainly used to ferry passengers and cars across the English Channel and the Solent.

A Westland Sea King twin-engined helicopter landing on an aircraft carrier. This helicopter can be used for anti-submarine warfare or search and rescue work

A hovercraft

5 Radio and television

Marconi with some of his earliest equipment

'Children's Hour' on a crystal set

Radio

Radio, or wireless as it was called for many years, was not invented so much as discovered. In the 19th century, experiments were made in sending messages by means of electrical impulses, without the use of wires.

A young Italian named Marconi came to England where, with the help of Post Office engineers and a scientist, Sir Oliver Lodge, he took the lead in experiments which enabled him to send a radio message from England to France in 1899. Two years later, he sent radio signals across the Atlantic. Professor John Fleming invented the radio valve in 1904 and for the next few years radio was chiefly used to send signals in Morse code. It was much used by ships and also by both sides during the 1914–18 War.

From Morse code signals, it became possible to convert the sounds of human speech or music into electrical impulses which were sent from a studio to a powerful transmitter. These impulses were picked up by a domestic aerial linked to a wireless set, whose loud-speaker converted them into the original sounds of speech or music.

By 1920, the Marconi Company at Chelmsford was sending out occasional programmes for enthusiasts. The world's first broadcasting station was opened in Pittsburg in America, and, in 1922, a London station was started, with a call-sign 2LO. In the following year the British Broadcasting Company began sending out programmes from its studio at Savoy Hill, London. No other company was allowed to operate and the cost of broadcasting was met by licence fees paid by the owners of wireless sets. By 1926, 'wireless' was becoming part of everyone's home life.

In 1927, the British Broadcasting Company become a Corporation, with a Royal Charter, a group of governors and a Director-General, Sir John Reith. BBC programmes for schools began in this year.

*The 'wireless saloon'
on a railway train, 1923*

Early wireless sets had no valves but a 'crystal', a thin piece of quartz or carborundum, on which rested a wire, called the 'cat's whisker'. You had to tickle the cat's whisker to tune in; because the sound was very feeble, people put on earphones to 'listen in'. There was a great deal of crackling and interference, and the tall wireless pole in the garden carrying the aerial was sometimes blown down or struck by lightning. Wireless sets with valves replaced the crystal sets; these required a large battery and an 'accumulator' which had to be recharged every week at a wireless or cycle shop. Mains sets were a great advance on the battery types. Many people built their own sets and newspapers carried articles telling enthusiasts the best ways to get good results.

Tickling the cat's whisker—this crystal set cost 7s 6d in 1924

Portable radio set, described as 'compact enough to be carried anywhere and only requires switching on to hear the programme'

Portable sets and car radios came in from about 1930, and the 1960s saw the arrival of the valveless transistor set, which was about a tenth the size of the old cabinet model.

By 1932, the BBC had left Savoy Hill for Portland Place; regional stations had been set up in other cities and programmes were broadcast to Europe and the Empire.

During the Second World War, the Forces' programme was introduced to entertain troops and workers; then, in 1945, came the Home Service and the Light Programme, with more serious broadcasts on the Third Programme from 1946. These names were changed in 1967, when the Home became Radio 4, and Radio 1, 2 and 3 were introduced.

Broadcasting House

Studio broadcast of Shakespeare's play 'Othello'

Television

As early as 1908, a scientist named Campbell-Swinton proved that light impulses could be transmitted and received by a cathode-ray tube. Little further was done until a Scot, John Logie Baird, devoted himself to the problems of sending and receiving light signals. Almost penniless, he continued his work and in 1920 he demonstrated 'radio-vision' in London and his apparatus was on show in the Wembley Exhibition of 1924. Four years later he actually transmitted pictures from London to New York and this triumph led to his being engaged by the BBC. The world's first television service started in November 1936 from Alexandra Palace, on a hill in London.

At this time, the very short wavelengths used by television were only effective for about 50 km from the transmitting station. Screens were very small, reception was poor and watchers had to sit in complete darkness.

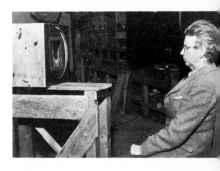

John Logie Baird

A radiogram/ television set presented to HRH Princess Elizabeth (the Queen) at her wedding in 1947

The first televised boat race, 1938. Oxford won

*Making up an actor
for colour television*

During the war programmes ceased but a great deal was learned about radar and this knowledge helped to improve television when broadcasting was resumed in 1946. Larger screens arrived, interference from nearby electrical machinery was reduced and more and more people began to buy or hire television sets. All programmes at this time were in black and white. Unlike sound broadcasting there was an alternative to the BBC, for, in 1955, the first commercial programme came on to the screen.

From 1961, the American communications satellite *Telstar* reflected signals, so that programmes could be received from across the Atlantic and it became possible to watch events taking place in, say, New Zealand or Mexico. Baird had shown that colour television was a possibility, but this was not developed until 1953 in America and some years later in Britain. A colour service became available to much of Britain from 1967.

Filming a ball scene for War and Peace

Rich and poor 6

Hunting in the Edwardian period

The contrast between the lives of the rich and the poor was far greater in Edwardian times than today. With income-tax low and servants cheap, the rich were able to live extremely well. The fashionable class, at whose head stood Edward VII, could devote themselves to pleasure. The poor, on the other hand, worked long hours for wages which were generally so low that they and their children were ill-nourished, ill-clad and poorly housed.

Owners of big country houses enjoyed holding weekend parties for their friends, when perhaps 40 servants cleaned and dusted the house, lit the fires, carried the coals, cooked the ample meals and looked after every need of the guests. As many outdoor servants tended the gardens and green-houses, groomed the horses, polished the carriages and probably learned to service the new car. The estate often included farms and a village, most of whose inhabitants worked for the owner of the 'big house' or depended to some degree upon his goodwill.

Black-leading a grate —one of many chores performed by servants

The lady of the village visited the poor, who depended on the goodwill of her and her husband

35

Lady Gort's house party at Cowes, 1912

Tennis in 1922 (above) and a party off to Henley in 1906

The rich spent their leisure shooting, hunting, attending the races and playing games like croquet and tennis, with billiards and whist indoors. There was dancing in the evenings and a great deal of eating and drinking. The year's round included the London 'season' of balls and theatre-going and regular events like Ascot, Henley, Cowes and shooting in Scotland. Visits were also made to Paris, Biarritz and to fashionable spas in order to drink the medicinal waters.

Anyone with an income of £600 could not aspire to such heights of luxury but he was nevertheless very prosperous. He would live in a detached house and would almost certainly employ two or three servants.

A room in the slums

Those earning between £3 and £10 a week—senior clerks, shopkeepers and a good many professional men, like doctors and solicitors—had to be more careful but they were comfortably off, for rents were low, and prices steady (bacon sixpence a pound, butter one shilling a pound, coal 18 shillings a ton, boots about six shillings a pair). They would certainly keep a maid to do the housework; one woman in three who worked was a domestic servant.

Below £3 a week, the great majority of the population of Britain lived in various degrees of poverty. Farm labourers were lucky to earn £1 a week, with a free cottage; in towns many cotton workers earned less than £1, regular dockers received £1 to £1 15s, casual labourers might earn 3s 6d a day. Engineering, ship-building workers and skilled craftsmen like cabinet-makers could make up to £2 a week.

Every moderately well-off family had at least one maid

37

Women were appallingly paid, with the maidservants getting about 7s 6d a week, while the girls in the East End of London factories making, say, corsets, brushes or umbrellas, earned 8 to 18 shillings.

What did such wages buy? The answer is never enough food and clothing to keep people healthy. A man named Seebohm Rowntree, who cared about the poor, worked out that if a wife was very very careful and never wasted a penny, and if her husband neither smoked or drank, they and their three children needed £1 1s 8d a week to live well enough to be able to work. Yet a tenth of the population of York had less than this sum and Rowntree reckoned that a quarter of the entire population was living in poverty.

That is why, in Edwardian times, sickly ragged children were always to be seen on the streets, why families lived in slums, why a disease of the bones called rickets, caused by lack of nourishing food, was commonplace and why, during the Boer War, nearly 40% (60% in some places) of recruits for the Army were turned down because they were not physically fit.

Seebohm Rowntree

Welfare

One of the great advances of the 20th century is that the tremendous contrast in the lives of rich and poor has been lessened. Poverty has not been entirely wiped out but large numbers of children no longer go ragged and hungry; people who are poor, sick or old can now receive help. How has this happened?

In 1908, Old Age Pensions were introduced in Britain for persons over 70; the sum was 5s 0d a week or 7s 6d for a married couple—not very much but enough to keep them from the dreaded workhouse. Minimum rates of pay were fixed for the worst-paid jobs and, in 1910, Labour Exchanges were opened to help the unemployed to find work. National Insurance (1911) provided a weekly income (10s 0d) for some workers while they were sick, with free medicine and medical attention. At the same time, unemployment pay was introduced for some, but not all, workers.

A queue of unemployed outside a labour exchange in 1924. Not enough work was available

Whitechapel, London in 1911

This was the beginning of what has been called the Welfare State. During the 1920s and 1930s, many people suffered because of widespread unemployment. There were usually between two and three million persons without a job and this meant that, counting their families, something like a quarter of the population in Britain had not enough to eat, had insufficient clothes, comfort and pleasures. Unemployment pay, called the 'dole', was low—about 29 to 36 shillings a week for a man, wife and three children—and a report of 1936 found that half the nation could be considered ill-fed. Hardship was worst in South Wales, the North of England and parts of Scotland.

A great deal has been done since World War II to improve the lives of those who need help. A politician named Beveridge had issued the Beveridge Report in 1942 to show how this might be done and the first step was the grant of Family Allowances in 1945. Next came the National Health Act of 1946, bringing in a system to provide medical care for everyone. Unemployment benefits and old age pensions were increased.

National Assistance was set up to help those who had special needs, such as old people with no income except their old age pensions or workers on short time. Help can also be given to disabled persons and to low-paid workers. These measures are not perfect, but for the old, the young and the unfortunate, Britain is without doubt a very much better place to live in today than in Edwardian times.

The first payment of the Old Age Pension, 1 January 1909

Soup kitchen, 1903

Houses 7

During the years between 1900 and 1914, upper-class houses became lighter and airier than Victorian homes and less cluttered with heavy furniture and ornamental knick-knacks. White paint took the place of brown, light-coloured wallpapers replaced the heavy reds and browns; verandahs and glass conservatories became popular and, in big houses, the kitchen tended to be on the ground floor instead of in the basement.

House of about 1900

Bathrooms were installed in quite modest middle-class homes, which were usually built in neat terraces, with tiny front gardens, just wide enough to set the house back from the street. A 1910 villa would be entered through a small porch into a narrow hall, from which the stairs led up to a dim landing off which were three bedrooms and the bathroom. Downstairs, one behind the other, came sitting-room, kitchen and scullery, the latter containing a gas-stove, shallow earthenware sink and a copper in which the weekly wash was done.

Typical town terraced houses about 1900 (left) and semi-detached houses of 1908 (right)

Water was heated by the black kitchen range and the rest of the house made do with coal fires in one or both of the living-rooms. Fires were only lit upstairs in case of illness. The small back-gardens sometimes contained a wash-house but there was no provision for a garage because no one thought that middle-class persons would ever own one of those new-fangled motor cars.

The workers mostly lived in meaner versions of this type of house. Thousands of terraced streets had been built in Victorian times, containing rows of houses with two rooms upstairs and two down, with an outside privy and a cold tap in the kitchen. Some of the terraces were neat and trim but many were falling into the ruinous state that made them into slums.

The worst slums were the 'back to back' houses, double rows of mean dwellings, their front doors facing on to narrow alleys in which stood the privies shared by many families. There were no back doors because, for cheapness, a single wall divided the two rows.

In the slums (above, right) modern conveniences, such as Ewart's patent geyser with shower attachment (above), were not found
At Port Sunlight (left), better working class housing had been built in the 1890s.
But the houses on the right were still standing in 1974

In hope that workers might live in better surroundings, a man called Ebenezer Howard wrote a book called *Tomorrow* and this led to the founding in 1903 of the first garden city, Letchworth in Hertfordshire. Its houses were arranged in crescents, closes or groups of four; most had indoor sanitation, a hot water system and a bath. There were gardens and greenswards, a shopping area, various public halls (though no public houses) and a factory area that was separate but not too far from the houses.

This venture has influenced the design of workers' houses and the layout of housing estates down to the present day.

Letchworth Garden City from the air

Ribbon development. People liked houses by the side of main roads because they could easily catch a bus, and the noise of traffic was much less than now

After the First World War, there was a great housing shortage, so the Government directed councils to put up houses to let at low rents and there was also a boom in private building. Most of the new houses had to be built on the outskirts of existing towns, so suburbs extended farther and farther into the country and a great many houses were built on either side of the roads leading out of town. This is called ribbon development.

Most of the new houses were cheap, costing between £500 and £800, and far too many were extraordinarily ugly. However, they did have electricity, main sewerage and bathrooms. Bungalows became popular, because they were cheaper than a house and were particularly suitable for young couples and retired folk. One fashion which had a vogue for a time was the flat-roofed 'ultra-modern' house that looked rather like a white sugar cube.

Council house 'boxes', an ugly bungalow, and an 'ultra-modern' house of the 1930s

Once again, war put an end to house building and, when peace came, there was a shortage of houses. Prefabricated homes were made in factories, mostly from asbestos sheeting, and were quickly assembled on their sites. These pre-fabs were squat and unlovely but they served a need and their kitchens were better designed than any in pre-war houses.

Pedestrian precinct at Stevenage New Town

By this time, it was no longer possible for a man to build a house where and how he liked; he had to get planning permission, which was necessary to prevent bad standards and to preserve the countryside. A number of new towns were built and large extensions were added to existing towns. Ebenezer Howard would have been pleased to see that these big housing projects were carefully planned so that they had their own factory and shopping areas, spaces for recreation and houses grouped in more interesting ways than straight lines.

A pre-fab, built about 1947 and still standing (left) and houses in a new town

Three typical kinds of housing in the 1970s

Architects tried to avoid monotony, so the houses were varied. Some were built of brick, others of concrete; some had timber facings or were tile-hung; gables might face the road, roofs might be almost flat or single-pitched. Terraces came back, but garages were not forgotten and these were often built in groups a short distance away. Windows became much larger; outside walls were often colour-washed and doors painted in bright colours.

In large cities, shortage of land led to the building of multi-storey flats. 'High-rise' building, as it was called, created problems, because people often felt isolated and mothers, living high up, were reluctant to let small children go to play out of their sight. As a result, tall blocks of flats are now only built in a few of the biggest cities, especially London, Glasgow and Southampton, and are interspersed with 'medium-rise' blocks of up to eight storeys.

Inside the home

In recent years, a housewife's work has become less laborious, through the introduction of new foodstuffs, like breakfast cereals, fish-fingers and canned vegetables, new materials like drip-dry shirts and plastic tiles, and machines like refrigerators and washing-machines.

Some of these labour-saving devices are not new; a bellows-type hand-worked vacuum cleaner came on the market in about 1908 and an electric type in 1917. Gas cookers, electric light, refrigerators and washing-machines of a sort go back to Victorian times; electric cookers were available from about 1920, but until the 1930s or later the vast majority of housewives had never seen these novelties and could not afford them.

In most homes, the dustpan and brush, broom, bucket and scrubbing-brush were all that were used to keep the house clean; carpets were taken outside to be beaten, stone or tiled floors were scrubbed by hand, front door-steps were hearth-stoned every morning, brass taps and door knobs polished with metal polish, knives cleaned in a special knife machine and the forks and spoons polished with plate powder.

An electric iron (left) and the fully electric kitchen, both 1896— but electric kitchens were very rare until the 1930s

A 'system for the supply of hot and cold water throughout a residence' dating from 1892

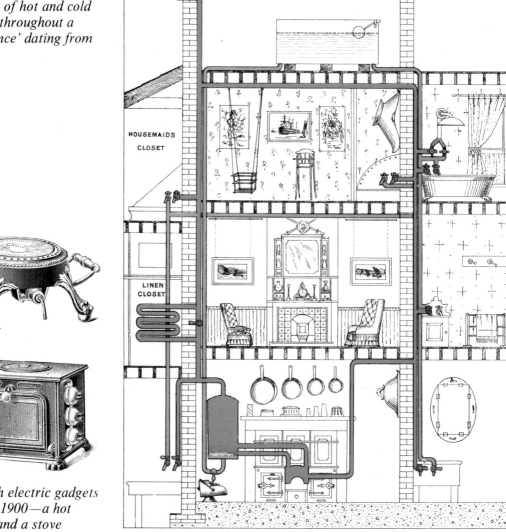

HOUSEMAIDS
CLOSET

LINEN
CLOSET

French electric gadgets about 1900—a hot plate and a stove

Many homes were lit by gas or, in the country, by oil-lamps, until electricity became available to almost everyone after World War II.

Coal fires caused a great deal of work—black-leading grates, laying fires, carrying coals, dusting and polishing— and this has been reduced by the introduction of smokeless fuels, of solid fuel stoves and of central-heating systems, worked by gas, oil or electricity. Warmer homes have led to 'open-plan' designs, with as few internal walls as possible to give a feeling of spaciousness.

Washing day—a picture from a nursery rhyme book

The greatest changes have taken place in the kitchen where, until about the 1920s, the cast-iron range warmed saucepans on its top, roasted joints in its oven and heated the water in a side boiler. Many homes had no other means of cooking, but gas stoves, also black, were quite common by 1914. A device called 'Regulo' to control gas pressure made cooking easier, but electric cookers were not widely popular until after the Second World War.

Wash-day was usually Monday, when the copper fire was lit and the clothes were boiled in hot soapy water, rubbed on a washing-board, rinsed and hung out to dry. Ironing was done with flat-irons heated on the stove and constantly changed, though there were box-irons in which glowing charcoal could be placed. Gas-irons with a flexible tube to the gas-tap were invented in 1880 and electric irons before the First World War, but, like so many new devices, they did not enter ordinary homes until some twenty or thirty years later.

Electric toaster (left) and grill for steaks, about 1900

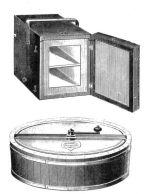

An ice-cave, made of wood lined with tin, and Marshall's Patent Freezer ('produces delicious ice within 3 minutes') costing £5 for the one gallon size

Kitchens became easier to work in between the wars, probably because the middle-class housewife had to do her own housework when servants had become scarce and expensive. In new houses, the kitchen was lighter and more convenient, with flat work-tops and a kitchen cabinet in place of the old open dresser. The sink became deeper and was provided with a wooden draining-board; walls were tiled and a hot water system was installed.

After the Second World War, the kitchen was often the best-designed room in the house. Stainless steel sinks and mixer taps were fitted, a range of units would include a refrigerator, the gas or electric cooker, a washing machine and sometimes a dish-washer as well. Wall cupboards provided storage space and because the 'fridge took care of foods like milk and meat, a separate larder with its cool shelf was no longer needed.

The kind of kitchen which advertisers would like us to have in the 1970s. Not many houses have a kitchen like this!

50

Cinema 8

By the end of Queen Victoria's reign, moving picture shows were being given to the public. These were usually comic turns, boxing matches or realistic scenes like a train arriving at a station. The cinematograph seems to have been invented by an Englishman named Friese-Greene, but it was an American cameraman who first had the idea of telling a story in pictures; and in 1903 he made *The Great Train Robbery*, the first real film.

This was a sensational success and, within a few years, companies were producing films and empty shops and halls were being turned into cinemas. An English music hall comic named Charlie Chaplin went to America in 1910 where he made several short films for the Keystone Company.

The 1914–18 War put an end to film making in Europe, and America took the lead. California's warm sunny climate was ideal for outdoor 'shooting' and a place called Hollywood became the acknowledged centre of film-making. G W Griffiths made two brilliant films there, *The Birth of a Nation* (1915) and *Intolerance* (1916), for which he used great crowds and spectacular scenes.

Charlie Chaplin in Gold Rush

Modern Times, with Chaplin and Chester Conklin

Mickey Mouse

Mary Pickford

In the 1920s, the star system developed, with screen heroes and heroines like Rudolf Valentino, Douglas Fairbanks and Mary Pickford ('the world's sweetheart'). The fascinating Greta Garbo arrived towards the end of this period but most beloved of all the stars was Charlie Chaplin, appearing in *The Kid* (1920), *The Gold Rush* (1925) and *The Circus* (1928).

The arrival of talking pictures in 1927, with Al Jolson in *The Jazz Singer*, brought fantastic prosperity to the cinema industry. In the 30s, going to the pictures became a weekly event for most families. They enjoyed mammoth 'double feature' shows (plus a live stage show in many places) for as little as sixpence or a shilling. Cinemas became vast luxurious palaces, decorated in exotic styles and throbbing with the subdued music of the cinema organ played by a resident organist.

Hollywood produced an endless stream of musicals, comedies, gangster films and tragedies, and the stars are almost too numerous to mention, except perhaps the Marx Brothers, dancers Fred Astaire and Ginger Rogers, Clarke Gable, Gary Cooper, Spencer Tracy and Mickey Mouse.

Rudolph Valentino as The Sheik

On location

52

Cinema interior, 1930

The cinema kept its hold on the public throughout the Second World War and well into the 50s until television dealt it almost a knockout blow. In 1948 people made some 28 million visits a week to the cinemas of Britain; by 1968 the figure was down to below three million. The once-opulent 'Palaces' and 'Majestics' stood forlorn and empty, and many towns no longer possessed a single cinema. There are still some fine films being made, many of them in Italy, France and Britain, but the glamour and excitement of cinema-going in the 30s has disappeared.

The Granada, Tooting, in Gothic style 1931 (above) and the news theatre at Victoria, 1933

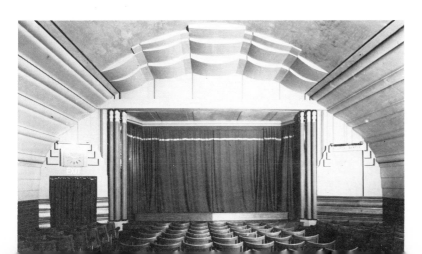

9 Railways

Great Central 4–4–0 locomotive, 1920

Lancashire & Yorkshire railway 2-4-2T, originally introduced in 1889

The coming of the motor car did not seem likely to threaten the all-powerful railway companies. There were more than a hundred of these, nearly all of them doing well, for everyone travelled by rail and every ton of coal, foodstuffs and merchandise had to be conveyed from the mines, docks, and factories by goods trains.

The locomotives were of course steam-powered, and the trains ran with efficiency and speeds that compare favourably with today's services.

In 1921, all the railway companies were reduced to four: the Great Western Railway (GWR), the London, Midland and Scottish (LMS), the London and North Eastern Railways (LNER) and the Southern Railway. Each retained its distinctive colours for the carriages. During the interwar years there were improvements in passenger comfort, such as corridor trains, dining and sleeping cars. There were still three classes of travel, 1st, 2nd and 3rd class, though 2nd class tended to die out.

The Mallard achieved a world record 126 mph in 1938

The companies took pride in the performance of their crack locomotives including the *Flying Scot* and *Mallard,* which broke the world's speed record in 1938, reaching 126 mph (202 km/h) between Grantham and Peterborough.

On 1 January 1948, the four companies were nationalised and all their property, track and rolling stock became British Railways, later known as British Rail. The post-war period has seen the end of steam, as diesel locomotives have taken over from the splendid snorting monsters with their great driving wheels.

The diesel engine, invented by Dr Rudolf Diesel in 1897, has several advantages over its steam counterpart; it is less costly to run and does not require so much cleaning and maintenance; it can be ready for work at a moment's notice instead of having to stand for hours getting up steam. It is in fact an internal combustion engine, i.e. its fuel (oil) is burned in the cylinders and not in a separate boiler as in the steam locomotive.

The last run of British Rail's last standard gauge steam train

Locomotive 70013, named Oliver Cromwell

A narrow gauge locomotive at Aberystwyth

A typical 0-6-0 diesel shunter of the 1950s

A poster advertising rail freight

The Brighton Belle (right)

A Freightliner terminal

The driver's view at 160 km/h

Electricity has been used to drive trains on London's Underground since the 1890s and in recent years, electrification using overhead wires has been extended to many suburban British Rail services.

Constant improvements have been made to tracks, signalling systems, stations, passenger and goods services, yet the railways continue to lose vast sums of money. A great many unprofitable lines have been closed down (some people think too many), so that British Rail can concentrate on the heavy 'commuter' traffic of the big cities, on container trains and fast inter-city services.

Cars, lorries, and aeroplanes make it difficult to run a railway profitably, yet a country like Britain with its overcrowded roads, cannot afford to let its railways go out of existence.

Ships 10

Early in the 20th century, Britain's navy, by far the most powerful in the world, was challenged by Germany. To keep her lead, Britain produced HMS *Dreadnought* in 1908, the first of a class of super battleships. She had 12-inch guns, armour-plating, torpedoes and wireless and was powered by steam turbines. Since she made all other battleships obsolete, Britain and Germany became rivals, each nation trying to build more battleships, cruisers, destroyers and submarines than the other.

Navies continued to develop between the wars, when aircraft-carriers came into service, providing fleet commanders with the means to seek out the enemy, to track his movements and attack his ships from the air. In addition to great carriers like the *Ark Royal*, smaller aircraft carriers were built to protect convoys from surface and submarine attack. A British invention called Asdic was fitted to warships to enable them to detect submarines under the water.

Since World War II, most of the huge battleships and aircraft-carriers have been scrapped, because the most powerful naval weapon is now the missile-carrying nuclear-powered submarine.

HMS Dreadnought,
1908 (top) and
HMS Howe, 1942

Explosion aboard the
British submarine A.5
in 1905

The past seventy years have seen the heyday and the decline of the great ocean liners. Perhaps the most famous of these was Cunard's *Mauretania* (30 695 tons gross), built in 1907. For 20 years, 1909–1929, she held the Blue Riband, an imaginary award for the fastest crossing of the Atlantic. This splendid ship with her luxurious cabins and saloons for wealthy passengers, set the style for a whole class of liners which appeared between the wars.

Other famous liners included the German *Bremen* and *Europa,* the Italian *Rex* and the French *Normandie.* In 1936, the *Queen Mary* made her maiden voyage, to be followed by the *Queen Elizabeth* in 1940 during wartime. Both the 'Queens' were so fast that they could be used as troopships without naval escort. After the war these great ships, both over 80 000 tons, carried thousands of passengers to and from America.

Servia, 1881

Mauretania, 1907

Queen Elizabeth, 1940

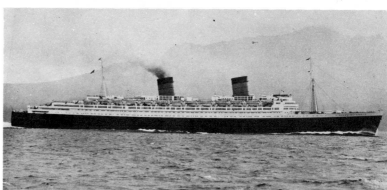

Queen Elizabeth II, 1969

But the day of the luxury liner, with its wonderful public rooms, swimming-pool, dance hall and tennis courts, is nearing its end, except for holiday cruises. The development of jet aircraft has drastically reduced the number of passengers who want to spend the extra time and money on a sea-crossing. The Americans have practically abandoned the North Atlantic route and the Italian liner fleet is destined to be broken up. Britain still operates the *Queen Elizabeth II*, but for how long?

One of the most remarkable developments in shipping has been the appearance of the giant oil tankers. These monsters, developed after the closing of the Suez Canal in 1956, have become so vast that there are only a few ports in the world at which they can call. Many are over 300 metres long and of more than 100 000 tons gross. In 1972, the world's largest ship was the 480 000-ton tanker *Globtik Tokyo*, but even bigger ones have been ordered.

The nuclear submarine HMS Dreadnought

A modern oil tanker, serviced at sea by a helicopter

59

11 Medicine

Medical science has made such progress during the 20th century that people live longer and are much healthier. Many diseases and illnesses which were formerly serious have been brought under control.

Much of this progress has been through the development of immunisation (protection against illness through injecting into the body a harmless form of the disease) and of better vaccines, which are materials which are injected into the body. Professor Almoth Wright used immunisation to protect Boer War soldiers against typhoid; this was used much more widely in the 1914–18 War and, with a similar injection for tetanus (lockjaw), thousands of lives were saved.

Diphtheria, a disease attacking the throat, was often fatal in children, until the British government started a campaign for immunisation in 1940.

Vaccination in 1894 and today

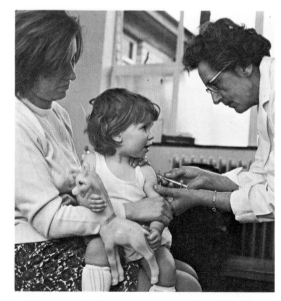

From the 1930s, drugs known as sulphonamides were produced, to check the growth of germs (bacteria). A Scottish doctor named Alexander Fleming discovered penicillin in 1929, a drug which proved to be a powerful destroyer of bacteria. Another drug produced in the 1940s, was streptomycin, which is valuable in treating tuberculosis. Poliomyelitis (infantile paralysis) was specially dreaded, because it often left victims partly or completely paralysed. Alarming outbreaks occured in England in the 1950s, but the Salk vaccine, produced in America, seems to have almost wiped out the disease.

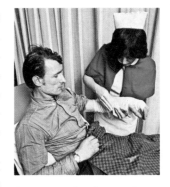

Putting a broken arm in plaster

Preventing disease

People are healthier today because they are generally better fed. Since about 1910, scientists have discovered more about the substances which make up our food— carbohydrates, proteins, fats and vitamins. We know that we need a balanced diet and that vitamin A (which is found in fresh milk, butter, egg-yolks and spinach) is necessary in order to grow, and that vitamin C (found in fruit and greenstuff) helps to prevent skin troubles.

Life is healthier, too, because, unlike conditions a century ago, most houses are provided with proper drains, flush lavatories, wash-basins and baths. Food shops, dairies and slaughter-houses have to be tested and inspected to make sure that they are clean and germ-free.

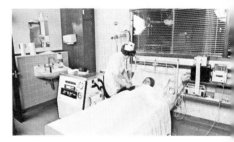

Three views in the newly rebuilt Charing Cross Hospital, Fulham

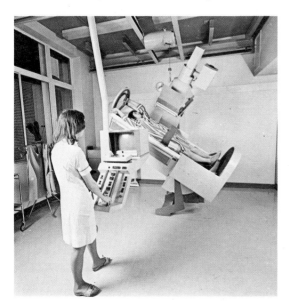

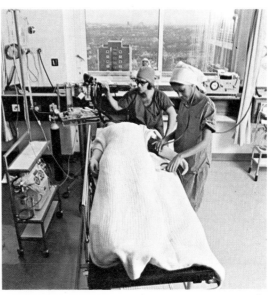

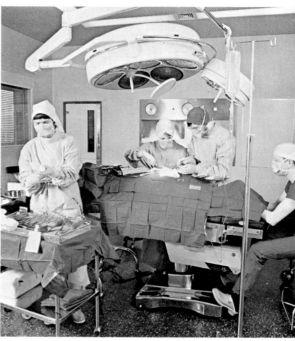

Operating theatre at Charing Cross Hospital in 1901 (left) and in 1973 (right)

Surgery

Since Joseph Lister made surgery much safer by using carbolic acid sprays in Queen Victoria's reign, there have been some amazing advances. Surgeons started using fine rubber gloves from the early 1900s and a little later, white gowns, masks and caps. High-pressure steam sterilisers have made instruments and dressings 'surgically clean', while air-conditioners maintain a supply of purified air.

New anaesthetics have replaced the old ether and chloroform, and a modern development is the use of *hypothermia*, or putting the patient into a 'frozen sleep'. This enables surgeons to carry out delicate operations on the heart and brain. All miracles seemed to be eclipsed in 1967 when in South Africa, Professor Christian Barnard replaced the heart of a 56-year-old man with that of a young woman.

Plastic surgery—the repair of people disfigured by burns or wounds—owes much to Sir Harold Gillies and his pupil Sir Archibald MacIndoe, who, in two world wars, developed techniques which enabled thousands of injured servicemen and civilians to return to normal life.

To sum up 12

A man who was born in 1900 and still alive in the 1970s could say that there had been more changes during his lifetime than in all the previous centuries of recorded history.

Cars and aeroplanes have transformed travel, so the world seems much smaller. It is also more crowded and polluted. Radio, television and films and popular sport have brought more entertainment to people's lives. All kinds of inventions and labour-saving devices have made work easier and most people have more leisure in which to enjoy themselves.

Two world wars brought tremendous changes, especially to Europe. Several empires have disappeared, including the British Empire, and Britain is no longer so powerful as in Edward VII's reign. Since Britain has joined the Common Market, she is linked more closely to Europe and this may bring additional changes.

To many people, life seems to be more hectic and less settled than in former years; prices and wages constantly rise and there is more violent crime. But, generally speaking people are better housed, better fed and better educated than ever before in history, and there is more concern for the old, the very young and those who are unfortunate.

City streets today (top) and Manchester in Edwardian times

Index

Index to the complete volume

The numbers in bold type stand
for the parts of *Looking at
History*. If, for example, you
look up *balloons*, you will find
that there are references to
pages 47 and 73 of Book **4**,
and to page 26 of Book **5**.